# COMEBACK

## EPIC REBOUND STRATEGIES FOR BUSINESS OR PERSONAL ADVERSITY

TODD BURNHAM

*Comeback* is published by Sutton Hart Press, llc
Vancouver, Washington

Inquiries: Inquiries@SuttonHart.com
Website: www.suttonhart.com
First Printing: September, 2022


ISBN
Hardcover: 978-1-947779-33-4
Digital: 978-1-94779-34-1

Library of Congress Number: Pending

Printed in the United States of America
Media and Reviewer Contact: maggie@platformstrategy.com
Copy Editor: Veronica Pamoukaghlian
Layout Design: Jason Enterline

# CONTENTS

# DEDICATION

*To the women who shaped my life.*

*To Nancy, my mom, for teaching me how to live.*

*To Katy, my wife, for teaching me how to love.*

*To Mae and Clara, my daughters, who continue to inspire me to be a better person.*

*And to Stephanie Randall, my friend, for believing in me when nobody else did.*

*Mahalo nui*

# INTRODUCTION

Staring at a gouge in the ceiling of his prison cell, Marco is tossing around methods for ending his life. He'd graduated Harvard Law, become a high-profile international financial consultant. By age 41, he'd traveled the Far East, married, had two kids, bought a multimillion-dollar Los Altos mansion, owned some Picassos, wrote a book, even summited Mount Everest. Ten years later, he's serving hard time for arson and insurance fraud. To him, it's over.

In the next cell over, 48-year-old Ryan is toweling off after his second HIIT session. He flips through the draft of his novel-in-progress, scribbles a note, chuckles at his clever idea. The Denver Law grad and former Colorado state court judge unfolds a neon inmate shirt, in awe of how quickly he's transformed his physique.

These guys screwed up. They worked their entire lives to build what they had – loving families, wealth, career success. And, true to form, mistakes charged in and reduced it all to ruins.

History is full of these stories, of great successes becoming even greater or totally derailed after a traumatic experience – whether it be a fatal business decision, a debilitating medical diagnosis, domestic abuse, a difficult divorce, the loss of a loved one. Some can't see a way out and spiral downward. Others seek a way out and find it, even using the traumatic experience itself as a launching pad.

Spending was Marco's fatal flaw. Millions of dollars in debt, he was busted for setting up an illegal lottery. He lost his license to practice, started drinking heavily, decided his best bet was to burn his mansion down for the insurance money.

Ryan's downfall was geniality. At the highest point in his career, he casually mentions a warrant he's working on to a friend. The friend tells a friend, who tells a friend that happens to be listed in the warrant. Ryan is disbarred and arrested for obstructing a federal investigation.

I spoke to Ryan the day before he went to prison. Of all things, he asked: "What kind of diet do you think they'll serve in commissary?"

"What do you mean?"

"Man, I'm coming out of this shredded, in better shape than ever."

Ryan was an excellent lawyer, one of the most genuine, authentic, good human beings I've ever worked with. He had a wife and three kids he adored, loved his work, and leveled up to State Court Judge by age 48 – a rare feat. But his incredible resilience was more impressive to me than all his accomplishments combined.

One of the most resilient people I've ever known is my mother, Nancy. I remember a specific moment from my childhood when I first came to appreciate her tenacity. I was walking to school, seventh grade, when a couple of kids approached me. They asked for money. One pulled out a knife. I gave them a dollar (all I had). Alarmed and shaken, I went back to tell my mom what happened.

At the time, mom was a social worker. She cared for troubled kids, those who were abused or neglected and had behavioral issues. She knew how important environment was to child development. She knew I had been acting out in school, getting in fights, and now I'd been held up at knife point.

To Nancy, protecting her son and giving him the tools he needed to thrive in this world was priority. But, as with most American parents, she didn't have the financial means to provide everything a parent wants for their child. We lived in The Valley, a rough neighborhood in the South Side of Syracuse where people worked hard and nothing was handed to you, where grit and grime and survival and street smarts are ground into the fibers of every kid's being.

But something in my mom switched once she learned of the knife incident. Desperation set in, a diehard resolve to make a change for her family. She went into survival mode. She became fixed on moving to a safer environment and would not be denied, money or no money. And I saw it. I was old enough to recognize it. It stuck with me for the rest of my life.

She borrowed money from people she didn't even know, and we moved to Fayetteville, New York, a working-class neighborhood in an affluent suburb of Syracuse and a hotbed for lacrosse. Most of the kids had played lacrosse since elementary school, but I caught on quick and ended up playing All-American. Fayetteville and lacrosse changed life as I knew it. My peers were talking about setting goals, winning games, going to college, all new concepts to me. They talked about team mentality, about practice and determination. It was in Fayetteville that I learned about opportunity.

Nancy's resilience ultimately changed her situation. Without desperation, she would not have considered such a move. My South Side years taught me survival, how to speak up for myself, how to play hard ball, all essential skills in today's world. Life in Fayetteville taught me drive, practice, determination, and opportunity, things I may or may not have picked up had we stayed put. All of it made me who I am today. Most importantly, my mother's actions taught me the value of desperation, and how it can fuel your drive to create change. When you want something bad enough, you get it.

Whether we like it or not, adversity and trauma are integral to the human experience. We all make bad decisions. We all fall into bad luck. We all suffer loss. And every one of us lies somewhere in the spectrum of two extremes in the way that we react. Some choose to lie down and forfeit. Others take the loss, buckle down into brand new plans, and shift direction toward a new and greater horizon.

So why does one person sway one way, toward hopelessness and despair, while the other sways the opposite direction, toward new focus, power, and greatness?

As a divorce lawyer, I've worked with thousands of people who are right smack in the midst of adversity or trauma, often the worst they've faced in their lives. And after more than a decade of working closely with this vast pool of people, each for months to years at a time, I stumbled upon a pattern. Across the board, those who pulled out of adversity to become better than they were before had six traits in common.

I wasn't looking for these commonalities, not specifically. As most divorce lawyers know, this job is disturbing, traumatic in itself. We step into a person's life at their worst, most painful moments. We see their very real concerns over losing their children, losing their homes, losing their businesses. We live it with them. And once the case is over, it's over. Our client loses maybe the only support system they've had for the past year, and we're expected to leave them abruptly with little to no tools for survival.

Years of the job took its toll. The only way I could face another day in this career was to ensure we made a lasting difference in the lives of our clients, make sure we didn't leave them high and dry, that their time with us actually improved their lives.

The question then became, how? Give them a housekeeper, nanny, therapist, pharmacist? A nice bank account? Sounds good on the surface, but like the old saying goes, give a man a fish and feed him for a day, teach him to fish and feed him for a lifetime. I wanted the latter. I wanted to bottle whatever those clients had, the ones who were able to survive and thrive after adversity. I devised an experiment. I compiled those six traits into six straightforward steps, then spent the next few years putting them into practice – both in my own life and in the lives of my clients and coworkers.

The result? Not only did the Six Steps help transform our client's lives, they helped transform the way I deal with the loss of loved ones, the way I handle addiction, the way I approach relationships, the way I parent, and the way our firm practices law.

Understand that this book is not intended as a replacement for mental health care. If you suffer from serious clinical depression, suicidal ideation, or other debilitating mental health issues, it is important to consult with professional outside help before moving forward. *See list of resources in Appendix.*

The tools in this book cannot be attributed to me, but to the thousands of people I've met throughout my professional journey that either gave up or made lemonade. Together, they taught me these valuable Six Steps. I've just listed them out.

# STEP 1: HIT BOTTOM

*"In their minds, people who turn trauma or adversity into success have no other choice."*

I no longer consider myself a divorce attorney. We're trauma lawyers. Many of the people my firm works with are going through the most difficult time in their lives, living through unbearable experiences, and getting through in the midst of trauma. They are no different than any of us. Around 70 percent of adults experience at least one traumatic event in their lifetime. Ten to thirty percent will develop post-traumatic stress disorder (PTSD). All of us, at one point or another, face some level of severe adversity.

I call this hitting bottom. You are in the midst of trauma, severe adversity, a life-changing event, experiencing a whole new level of fear and hopelessness. "Trauma" is hard to define, even controversial. Webster's defines trauma as "a disordered psychic or behavioral state resulting from severe mental or emotional stress or physical injury." The American Psychological Association defines trauma as "an emotional response to a terrible event like an accident, rape, or natural disaster." The DSM-5 of the American Psychiatric Association defines a traumatic event as "actual or threatened death, serious injury, or sexual violence." Social psychologists define trauma as an experience that shatters one's "assumptive world," their beliefs or assumptions about how people behave, how society functions, and what the future holds.

In short, there is no way to clearly define all the aspects of trauma, because trauma is in the eye of the beholder. I've hit rock bottom multiple times throughout my personal life and legal career, and I can tell you that "rock bottom" is relative. Worst case scenarios differ for everyone. All of them can be debilitating.

Losing a job may be no biggie for one person, but the end of another's world. One person may become suicidal over a breakup. Another person may think a felony arrest is the ultimate bottom. Many parents would call losing custody of their children their rock bottom. So, when we're talking about Step 1, hitting bottom, it's important to remember that it's all relative. You hit rock bottom when you, as an individual, believe you have hit the worst point of your life up to this point, regardless of what others would label as "trauma" or "adversity."

However you define rock bottom, it is a necessary state we must reach to be able to rocket ourselves onward and upward. A true comeback is not possible until you recognize you've hit an absolute low point.

CHAPTER 1

# SOME SINK, SOME SOAR

When I first came from New York to Colorado, our house was in foreclosure. A little adversity, right? I was under a lot of pressure to rebuild our financial lives and to succeed in my career as a Colorado attorney. Shortly after I was admitted to practice law in Colorado, I went to court, my first time in a Colorado courtroom. I went in thinking, "I've got this. I'm a New York lawyer. Nothing in Colorado compares to New York."

In walked a gentleman, a golfer type, tanned, with white slicked-back hair. He was pure confidence, joking around like he was best friends with others in the courtroom. This was the guy I was up against in my first case. The nerves kicked in. What the heck was I doing? And why did he have trial notebooks? And why didn't I have any? But I was determined not to be intimidated.

Everything was fine until this guy started interrupting me. I looked over at him, like, "Why do you keep interrupting me?" but he kept butting in as I was speaking. I became very frustrated. It was just rude. After a few more times of him interrupting me, I heard my mouth leak an aggressive, "Shhh!" I knew I was in trouble.

"Mr. Burnham," said the Judge.

"Yes, Your Honor?"

"We don't shush people in Colorado," he said. "I don't know where you're from, but that's not professional, and you're not going to have much of a professional life if you act like that in this court or any other court."

Needless to say, that sucked. I hadn't lost a job. I hadn't been diagnosed with a terminal illness. But I was a new lawyer in a new place with a new family, a house in foreclosure, and really needing for this new career move to work out. And I had just made a massive mistake on my first day at work. This Judge would remember I did this. The other attorney would tell all his colleagues. My reputation would boil down to "that jerk from New York who shushes other attorneys in open court." No one would respect me. Everyone would steer clients away from me. This new Colorado law practice of mine was going to completely tank.

This wasn't deep trauma; it was a little adversity – especially in hindsight. A "first-world problem." I am aware of the privilege I enjoy as a white male and U.S. citizen. My adversity looks very different than those of other cultures, races, and government structures. Every one of us experiences different levels of adversity. To many, this courtroom incident will seem trivial at best. However, it is important to recognize that – no matter our background – we are all human beings. To each of us, regardless of the details, adversity and trauma are painful and life-changing.

To me, the experience was devastating. Nobody died or was seriously injured or went to prison, but it was a severe trauma for me at that time in my life. The Judge's reprimand catapulted me into survival mode. I went home and promised myself I would never allow that to happen again. I told myself I was never going to be in a situation again where I (1) looked like an idiot and (2) acted like an idiot. I was going to take this experience and use it to build an extremely successful law practice just to prove to that lawyer and Judge that I was skilled and talented. I sat in my basement for six months and learned everything under the sun about Colorado family law. I adjusted my attitude, from an aggressive know-it-all to a nice guy just trying to do his absolute best. I suspect many will say that I remain an aggressive know-it-all, but I am/was just a guy going after the dream. I pushed hard to build a successful practice so that I would never feel my career was in jeopardy again.

What I couldn't possibly know is that I would use rock bottoms like these as launching points throughout my personal and professional career, carving out a life I could only dream of. I owe much of my success to many, many rock bottoms that allowed me to attack my life in a new way. Each disaster became a rung I placed my foot on to climb higher.

## Trauma Rips Away Your Safety Net

The professional adversity I experienced was trying, but trauma is often overwhelmingly devastating. When my friend Jaylen was a teenager, he came out to his religious, conservative parents. He had struggled with his identify for years and could no longer stand to deny his truth. His parents responded by kicking him out of the house and disowning him. He was now a young kid alone on the street with no money, no resources, and no support system. Jaylen's trauma was an all-encompassing rock bottom that exploded his world.

He had lost every sense of safety and security, his familiar surroundings were ripped away. But he had simultaneously gained an unbreakable strength in his truth and identity. Survival mode carried him through difficult experiences on the street and right into a new life. His rock bottom moment was the trigger that motivated him to create a successful life. Today he is a respected artist with a partner and son. He works with LGTBQIA youth organizations, offering other kids in his situation a safety net when they need it.

Jaylen's safety net was torn out from under him. Trauma can tear down our emotional, financial, physical, professional, and mental security. It is a destabilizing event that destroys the fabric of our reality, thrusting us into a deep dark hole we are certain we can never escape. And while my embarrassment in the courtroom seems to pale in comparison to Jaylen's experience, I can assure you both situations were traumatic. Again, "bottom" is in the eye of the beholder. I equate that gut-sinking feeling as a sign that the bottom is around the corner.

The trauma that brought you to this book was devastating for you, period. No matter what happened. And I am here to say you will come out better than before. If you feel you've hit bottom, you've already taken the first step. You're in survival mode – the fuel that drives rapid change. You've already begun to rebound. Add the next five steps and you'll end up crossing into a life greater than you can imagine.

If I had told Jaylen when he was a repressed teen hiding in his bedroom that one day he would be a successful full-time artist with a family of his own and a fulfilling life, he wouldn't have believed it. On the day his parents kicked him out, he wouldn't have believed the great things his future held. Little did he know, the trauma he went through was absolutely necessary for him to reroute his life and achieve his purpose, enriching others with his art and helping kids like him. Your trauma is necessary too. I know you don't believe it. I don't expect you to. But I can tell you good things are coming.

## Responses to Trauma

Like pro boxers, we all experience a knockout blow at some point. No matter how stable and unshakeable our world feels or how hard we work to achieve our goals, hitting bottom is inevitable. And like pro boxers, that knockout punch has the power to transform us into champions.

As humans, do we all respond similarly when that rock-bottom scenario happens? Scientists tell us that humans experience five stages of grief when we lose a loved one[1] – denial, anger, bargaining, depression, acceptance. It's a well-defined cycle with reams of data available in medical and scientific literature. Since trauma and adversity result in loss and grief, one would expect everyone to experience these stages, or at least a similar process. And we do. We make a mistake at work, get fired for it, try not to think about it, get raging mad, consider trying to get the job back, try to disappear in the bottle or sleep, and finally accept the new reality.

However, in following the lives of thousands going through trauma and having come out the other end, I noticed some important differences in the way individuals pass through each stage. The time they spend in each stage and the method they use to approach each stage varies from one individual to another. Take the depression stage; some will spend a month in bed, while others will spend the next ten years in an alcohol-induced delirium. Or the anger stage; some will break their hand punching a hole in the drywall, while others will spend their every waking hour plotting revenge.

No two people respond to hitting their rock bottom in the same way, but one important trend grabbed my attention. People's responses could be divided into two general categories. One group waved the white flag, surrendered to their new situation. Of course, time is a great healer, and most of these folks eventually mustered the strength to survive, to earn a living and perform their daily tasks again. But their potential fell by the wayside. They lost hope, couldn't get it back, accepted that the peak of their lives had come and gone.

Curiously, the other group of people faced with severe adversity skyrocketed to greater heights than before. Adversity challenged them, opened new doors, drove them down a brand-new path toward something more. While both groups went through the traditional stages of grief, this

1 Kübler-Ross, E. (1969). *On death and dying.* New York, NY: Macmillan.

second group came out even more productive and fulfilled than they were before the traumatic event. Why? Was it the severity of the trauma? Luck? Upbringing? Financial or educational privilege? Could I learn to develop this growth mindset myself?

## Why Different People React Differently

I started watching and listing factors that might play a role in these two very divergent reactions to adversity and trauma. What did all the success stories have in common? The obvious first guess was situation. The worse the problem, the harder it is to recover from, right?

But this was not always the case. Some people were professionals facing imprisonment, spouses dealing with severe abuse, or parents facing the loss of their children. Others lost their jobs, suffered life-changing injuries, or learned their partner was having an affair. To the outside observer, some problems seem much more traumatic than others. It's like that game, "Would You Rather?" One person might say they'd rather lose their job than be convicted of a felony, whereas someone else might rank things in a different way.

There are two reasons the specific situation doesn't determine the reaction to trauma. First, for each person I worked with who was going through hardship, their own problem was the end of their own individual world. All suffered equally and were just as devastated by the situation they were facing. Secondly, they each reacted to the situations in their lives differently. A woman who went to prison came out three years later with a bestselling novel and a new business, while a guy who lost his job started drinking, gained weight, and fell into a cycle of severe depression. It wasn't the severity of their situation that determined their reactions.

Did the answer lie in their brain chemistry? Maybe those who can't dig themselves out of a hole are genetically predisposed to depression, anxiety, fatigue, addiction, or an inability to handle difficult situations. Maybe some are born with a higher pain tolerance or are just more resilient. There's a lot of scientific evidence to show that these are important factors in how people do in life. But again, this factor didn't seem to determine which of the two categories a person fell into.

Some of the people I worked with had histories of mental health conditions, even as severe as generalized anxiety disorder, OCD, and bipolar disorder. But they managed to soar out of adversity. Others with those same histories completely fell apart. And some people with no history of mental health issues ended up drowning in their situations, while others with no history of mental health conditions came out of trauma more successful than before. Brain chemistry didn't seem to correlate with resilience in traumatic situations.

What about environment? Maybe people who can't get up from a fall were never taught to do so growing up. Maybe some were given better tools, a stronger foundation, a deeper support system, or a closer family, received a better education, a spiritual upbringing, or more money to block life's punches.

Again, no. Among the thousand-some people I worked so closely with over months and years, many who had strong support systems, solid foundations, and higher educations were knocked completely off track by severe adversity and never recovered. Others with similar backgrounds used the traumatic experiences to their advantage. And many of those who'd never finished high school, were brought up in abusive households, or had little financial stability, turned their challenge into an incredible boon, while others with these same environmental factors were unable to regain hope after trauma. None of these explanations worked.

## The Six Step Experiment

Finally, after a few years of careful observation, I was able to pinpoint six traits that those who benefited from adversity seemed to possess. Six traits that gave them the power to transform lemons into lemonade. In the minds of those with these six traits, trauma or adversity gave them no other choice than to bounce back **stronger**. Six traits seemed to define the group that soared.

I thought I would do a little experiment to determine whether those six traits could (1) be taught, and (2) increase the odds that a person would be able to turn tragedy into triumph. I took the six traits and listed them as Six Steps. I started drilling these Six Steps into the minds of coworkers, friends, family, and anyone who would listen, "Tony Robbins-ing" them (as they started calling it) into the notion that people who follow these Six Steps can turn any challenge—grief, betrayal, professional misfires, bankruptcy, loss—into powerful life changes. And then I watched.

## Bouncing Off the Bottom

Christopher was one of the first people who convinced me I had it right. He was a good man with a wife and two lovely kids. He came to us very distraught several years ago. His wife had filed for divorce. In her divorce petition, she'd filed a protective order alleging that Christopher regularly and frequently sexually abused his children. This was false. She was lying. And the accusation was completely and utterly devastating for Christopher.

Everyone can agree that being falsely accused of being a pedophile and child abuser is not your best day. As if it couldn't get worse, it does. Christopher was restricted from having any contact with his beloved children for three months while the legal process moved forward. And during those three months, his unstable wife was placed on an involuntary psychiatric hold—hospitalized without her authorization due to suicide concerns. There were no grandparents around. The kids had nowhere to go. For three months, they were placed in foster care due to the false allegations his wife had made against him.

This was Christopher's bottom, the worst thing to happen to him in his 36 years of life. He told me, "This is the worst thing I'm ever going to face in my life. Period. It completely sucks. My kids are with strangers, my reputation is on the line, and my family has been destroyed." He was stunned to find himself in the situation. I talked to him frequently about his mindset and counseled him on how to move forward. He listened.

Instead of panicking, floundering, or giving up, Christopher responded to the tragedy in an interesting way –with an immediate pivot. He recognized he had hit bottom, participated in the remaining five steps, and found himself suddenly obsessed with constructing a new life, deflecting attacks, and building a future. Christopher ended up with sole parenting rights. He escaped from his emotionally abusive marriage, is now thriving in his career, and is able to bring up his amazing kids in a healthy and fulfilling environment. He's happier and more successful than before the divorce. Funny, because while he was married, he thought he had it all. Little did he know that greater things were to come. Were it not for the traumatic accusations made against him, he may have never realized all that life had to offer.

But was it really a result of my "Tony Robbins-ing" this poor guy to death? Was I seeing the result of the Six Steps? At this point, all I knew was that the moment Christopher recognized he'd hit bottom, he became *hyper-focused* on embracing inevitable change. He acknowledged his life was the worst it could get and became obsessed with making it better.

Certainly, Christopher had the first of the Six Steps nailed down. He fully recognized he had hit rock bottom. He didn't try to ignore it. He couldn't. Adrenaline kicked in and started doing its job. Severe adversity had thrust him into survival mode.

We aren't talking mere worry or anxiety, but a recognition that you are facing the demise of your way of life. You've landed in a deep, dark hole and will do *anything* to get out. There is no other option. You fully recognize it. No denial. Think of it as the difference between hunger and starvation. When we're hungry, we might still turn down a raw egg or duck pâte. When we're starving, we'll scale a mountain for a grub worm. Without that level of drive, you're going to have a rough time climbing out of that hole. To change your life after trauma, you must first hit the absolute bottom. Rather, you have to get your mind right, convincing yourself that this is a dire situation (even if it's not).

Michael Jordan, the GOAT, famously created stories of disrespect in his mind in order to motivate himself. Jordan, and perhaps Kobe, are the greatest basketball players of all time. They were mindset masters. I suspect they convinced themselves they hit bottom daily.

## Remarkable Rebounds: Helen Keller

*"... Although the world is full of suffering, it is also full of the overcoming of it."*[2]

Helen Keller suffered an illness caused her to lose her sight and hearing before she turned age two. Her world turned silent and dark. She couldn't communicate or connect with the world around her. This was a rock bottom for her and her loved ones. When she was eight years old, her parents hired a teacher Annie Sullivan to work with her. She famously learned the sign for water when Sullivan made the symbol for water in her hand and held her other hand under water. Keller eventually learned to read, write, and speak. She became an outspoken advocate for the blind and deaf population and took up many other causes, becoming a founding member of the ACLU. She was an author, speaker, and inspirational figure who used her disability to inspire others and improve conditions and opportunities for those with disabilities. Keller's difficult beginnings pointed to a life of despair and hopelessness, but her will to survive, to communicate and create change, made her one of the world's best known success stories.

2 Keller H. (1903). *Optimism: an essay.* T.Y. Crowell and Company

CHAPTER 2

# SURVIVAL MODE: THE ULTIMATE SUPERPOWER

As humans, the desire to survive is our most powerful driving force, generating the highest form of focus. We do not experience this level of drive and focus until our own sense of survival is truly threatened, until we hit bottom.

Survival is not about wanting to succeed; it's about *needing* to succeed in order to survive. A hunger to succeed won't get you there, only life-threatening starvation is enough to push you forward. In their minds, people who turn trauma or adversity into success believe that they have no other choice. People who are drowning have zero concerns other than getting back on land. They don't care about their reputation, finances, or relationships. They are fully focused on a single goal. There are no distractions.

## Adversity Breeds Strength

When you're in the thick of a major life crisis, it can be hard to imagine how such devastation could produce a life better than before. But research[3] shows that adversity not only helps us change direction and move towards

3 Seery, Mark D., E. Alison Holman, and Roxane Cohen Silver. "Whatever does not kill us: cumulative lifetime adversity, vulnerability, and resilience." *J Pers Soc Psychol.* 99.6 (2010): 1025.

something greater, but it also makes us stronger and more capable of tackling future stressful situations.

Scars last forever. They create a permanent imprint. And trauma causes significant scarring. In one way or another, we are affected by traumatic situations for the rest of our lives. A majority of those who have come out of trauma thriving would still have preferred that the traumatic event never happened. The goal is not to avoid pain and suffering; that is an impossibility. The goal is to recognize the incredible power of growth that can result from traumatic events, to recognize serious adversity as a tool we can take advantage of and use to harvest immense benefits.

What adversity and trauma do to the mind is similar to what weightlifting does to the body. Lifting heavy weights tears the muscle, literally rips the microfibers, destroys them. "Feel the burn" they say. Weightlifters know they've made progress when they feel achy and sore in the days after a workout. During those few days of soreness, the muscle is repairing and rebuilding a larger, more powerful structure–allowing the weightlifter to eventually lift that same heavy weight with ease. Our bodies do not seek to build the torn muscle back to its former state. Instead, our bodies say, *okay, some serious heavy lifting is in my* environment *now; I'd better be able to handle it the next time.* So, while the previous muscle ripped and tore under a 100-pound weight, the new muscle thinks 100-pounds is a joke. Bring it on! In response to injury (ripped muscle fibers), the body (1) focuses on repair, and (2) morphs the previous state into a more powerful state.

Our bodies react in the same way with mental stressors. Trauma tears us apart, and our minds repair. Not to the state it was in before the trauma, but into a new and different state that will be able to handle that trauma the next time it comes around. The mind, like the weightlifter's muscle, is damaged by the trauma. It must rearrange itself into a new form that can handle that level of hardship. This "new form" may manifest as PTSD, severe anxiety, depression, obsessive-compulsive disorder, strength, power, resilience, or newfound optimism. The goal is to learn to manipulate your body and mind to adapt to trauma in a productive and beneficial way. This manipulation begins with one's ability to (1) recognize they are experiencing severe trauma, (2) recognize the power that lies behind it, and (3) recognize that they will never regain the life they had before the trauma. They are permanently changed.

During or after trauma, many people fail to embrace the all-important third component–that permanent change that trauma induces. Wound repair does not result in the same skin we had before. It is scarred. Torn muscle fibers do not repair to their previous state. They build an amplified, larger, more powerful muscle. And when we are injured by a traumatic event, we are permanently changed.

The biggest mistake I see people make in their journey through a traumatic event is trying to get back what they had *before* the event occurred. Trying to get their marriage back, their career back, their home, the life they once knew. As with muscle repair, getting *back* to where you were does not assist survival. We cannot survive if we do not adapt to our surroundings. To overcome serious adversity, we must both repair and *change*.

## Recognizing Rock Bottom

If you've picked up this book to learn how to get back what you had, you may want to keep browsing the bookshelves. "But I just want back what I had," some say. "I don't want to be more powerful or improved." That's fine. It just simply means you haven't hit rock bottom. Because when you hit bottom, you'll do anything to get out of it. You are drowning, and you'd easily trade life as you knew it for a chance to get out of the water. True survival mode is an entirely different kind of motivation. If change is necessary to get you there, your mind will be more than willing to make it happen.

For me, a new dad moving to a new state, starting a new career, responsible for not only my own life but now an entire family, the embarrassing courtroom incident was a knockout punch. It stunned me into survival mode, jolting me into immediate action. Burnham Law started in an unfinished basement in 2010. We now have seven offices, over forty attorneys, and nearly 100 employees. Sixty percent of our businesses is from referrals. I consider myself a professional lemonade maker.

When you hit your personal or professional bottom, what you had has disappeared. You have no choice but to create a new future. While you're doing it, you have to let go of what may happen, or what could happen. You're going in blind. All you know for certain is that you *will* become greater than before. It may take a complete career change, an entirely new living situation, you cannot predict what the future holds. In survival mode, none of that matters. Everything is equally impossible, and everything is equally possible. Survival mode opens up options you could never have considered before hitting bottom.

## Adversity Prompts Change

The beauty of trauma is that it erects a stop sign in your life. You're forced to stop and consider other plans. If you live a charmed life where everything flows along smoothly, you will just continue to float along, taking what comes your way. Only when life crashes down around you do you gain the opportunity to learn and grow and rebuild. Trauma is horrific. No one deserves to experience the pain and suffering adversity brings into our lives.

But trauma is inevitable for each and every one of us. No one is immune. It is vital that we learn how to capture the power that lies within pain and suffering, that we train our minds to use the traumatic experience in a way that benefits us and those around us.

## Trauma Changes Our Brain

The idea that great suffering brings great wisdom isn't a new one. Buddhists believe suffering is necessary to ethical development and spiritual awareness. In 458 B.C., the Greek playwright Aeschylus emphasized in his play *Agamemnon* how "wisdom comes alone through suffering" and "he who learns must suffer." Suffering leads to self-reflection,[4] and this kind of intense reflection and focus in turn creates wisdom. Maybe you had an older relative who was all about letting things "toughen you up." Turns out, they were on the right track.

Research over the past few decades is beginning to map out more specifically how adversity and trauma alter the human brain. For example, scientists have determined that the prefrontal cortex region of the brain (responsible for executive functions like memory, planning, inhibition, cognitive flexibility, and abstract reasoning) undergoes physical change with trauma.[5] That trauma that feels like it physically ripped your heart out? It makes a permanent mark on your brain too. It changes how you think. You'll never be the same.

According to researchers at the University of North Carolina at Charlotte, [6] trauma triggers post-traumatic growth (PTG) and positive psychological

4 Brady MS. Why Suffering Is Essential to Wisdom. September 2019. *J. Val. Inq.* 53(3).

5 Nakagawa, S., Sugiura, M., Sekiguchi, A. et al. Effects of post-traumatic growth on the dorsolateral prefrontal cortex after a disaster. *Sci Rep* 6, 34364 (2016).

6 Tedeschi RG, Calhoun LG. Posttraumatic Growth: Conceptual Foundations and Empirical Evidence. *Psychol. Inq.* 2004;15:1–18.

changes caused by a major life crisis. Studies found that PTG affects five general areas of human functioning.

- First, serious adverse events increase empathy, the ability to identify with others' hardships, inevitably leading to stronger relationships. When we have experienced the worst possible scenario in our own life, we are better able to understand how other people feel when they deal with adversity. This allows us to bond more strongly with others.

- Second, people who have experienced a major life crisis show an increased ability to detect opportunities and paths that were not previously visible. Rock bottom kicks us into survival mode, prompting us to seek ALL possible solutions and paths forward.

- Third, trauma induces an increased sense of strength–a feeling of "now I can get through ANYTHING." We develop a newfound confidence. The more difficult times we live through, the better equipped we feel to take on whatever else comes. In a way, it's like building job skills. The more problems we deal with in our jobs, the better we become at them. The more struggles we deal with in life, the better we become at life.

- Fourth, trauma can induce a greater appreciation for life in general. Once we've hit our rock bottom, we can see the good stuff in our lives more clearly and are more grateful to have the people, things, and experiences that make us happy and support us. This in turn makes it easier for us to rebuild after each successive trauma that we experience.

- Finally, study participants who had experienced a major life crisis exhibited some change or deepening in spirituality. Going through challenging events tends to make people become more spiritual. Spirituality, as will be discussed in a later chapter, is not religion. It is a deeper understanding of ourselves that can help us develop a more positive and realistic mindset as we move forward out of trauma.

Additionally, studies out of the University of British Columbia found that adults who experienced a major trauma, like divorce, death of a spouse, life-altering illness, or injury, showed a higher capacity for enjoying life's simple pleasures, promoting greater life satisfaction. Importantly, this benefit was seen among participants of all personality traits–meaning it can happen to anyone.[7]

These are very important impacts. Trauma makes us better able to connect to people and imagine paths forward. It makes us stronger and better able to appreciate life. You could say that people who survive trauma develop superpowers. The terrible, painful trauma we experience happens for a reason. Recognizing this is vital to harnessing the greatness that can result. Of course, none of us drowning in a traumatic event can see things this way. You feel like you simply do not have the strength to even get out of bed. Keep reading. You do!

## Knockouts Create Champions

Researchers at SUNY Buffalo[8] studying the effects of trauma found that,

7 Croft A, Dunn EW, Quoidbach J. From Tribulations to Appreciation: Experiencing Adversity in the Past Predicts Greater Savoring in the Present. *Soc. Psychol. Pers. Sci.* 2014;5(5):511-516.

8 Seery MD, Holman EA, Silver RC. Whatever does not kill us: cumulative lifetime adversity, vulnerability, and resilience. *J Pers Soc Psychol.* 2010 Dec;99(6):1025-41.

in addition to empathy and PTG, a major life crisis can build self-efficacy, a confidence in our ability to successfully deal with challenges. Getting through hard things makes us feel better able to handle whatever else life throws at us. Because we dealt with something awful, we know we can get through something else that is difficult. Just as our body rebuilds muscle to handle more weight, our brain changes to handle additional adversity.

This is the basis behind exposure therapy[9] where we cure a phobia by doing the terrifying act. For example, people afraid of public speaking who force themselves to speak in public eventually overcome their disabling fear. People afraid of heights who practice climbing ladders (starting with one step and gradually climbing taller and taller ladders) eventually reduce their fear of heights to manageable levels. They gradually train their brains to realize that standing in a high place does not cause injury.

Exposure therapy is *not* about throwing someone afraid of water into the pool, but gradually exposing them to it by talking about it, thinking about it, imagining being in the water, being near water, putting a toe in, then a foot, and so on. Trauma recovery works in this same gradual way. As we experience difficulties in life, we create new viewpoints, emerging more confident and resilient than before.

The same study also found that adversity and trauma improve our ability to see the silver lining, the hidden good inside a difficult situation. Trauma changes our brains to interpret stress as a challenge rather than a threat, causing a different choice in the fight or flight response. Instead of wanting to run, a person who was previously exposed to a traumatic event will face future stressful situations with boosted energy, focus, efficiency, resources, confidence, concentration, performance, and satisfaction. Sign me up!

9 Institute of Medicine. Treatment of PTSD: An assessment of the evidence. Washington, DC: National Academies Press; 2007.

## PTG vs. Resilience

Because post-traumatic growth (PTG) induces change, researchers consider PTG and resilience (the ability to withstand difficult things) as two very different responses to trauma. For decades, psychologists have considered resilience to be the best protection against post-traumatic stress disorder. But more recent research indicates that resilience merely allows us to repair and recover to the level we started at. For those with low resilience, PTG tends to emerge, not only repairing you, but rebuilding you into a stronger, more powerful being.

In a study of veterans who developed post-traumatic stress disorder (PTSD), psychologist Jack Tsai of the Yale School of Medicine found that [10] you cannot fix what isn't broken. People who have high resilience are not broken by adversity; they are less affected by trauma and therefore less likely to develop PTG. They don't grow mentally bigger and stronger. More resilient people were more likely to develop debilitating PTSD. Less resilient people were less likely. Traumatic experiences are more painful for those with low resilience, but this increase in pain produces more PTG and greater future success.

Resilience gives us the strength to withstand difficult things, but it can prevent growth and change. If we are not broken by a traumatic event, we will not change and grow in response to it. If strong winds blow one shingle off your roof, you simply replace it. If a storm takes a chunk of your roof with it, you have no choice but to get a whole new roof, one that is inevitably newer, better, and stronger than the old one.

This is the moment where you get to pat yourself on the back for hitting rock bottom. Resilience is great, but it's not what you need right now. Falling

10 Tsai J, Mota NP, Southwick SM, Pietrzak RH. (2016). What doesn't kill you makes you stronger: A national study of U.S. military veterans. *J. Affect. Dis.*, 189, 269–271.

apart is exactly what you need for your brain to grow and change and allow you to build a life that is immensely better than what you had before. The more resilient we are, the less likely we are to experience profound change. You know you have reached rock bottom when you lack resilience (another silver lining to the pain and suffering associated with trauma).

## Tragedy Is Not Comparable

You may have heard of the Holmes-Rahe Life Events Stress Scale.[11] This is a chart that ranks the stressors (divorce, death of a spouse, losing a job, moving, etc.) a person might encounter in life by their severity. The idea is that some life events create more stress than others, and if you tally up a high score for events that happened in your life in the last year, you've experienced a lot of stress and are more susceptible to illness because of it. The scale, by its very nature, seeks to compare and rate hard things. This can be helpful if you're feeling stressed but aren't sure why. In that situation, it can be useful to give you an indicator that you've gone through a lot and you should take care with your health.

However, this is not helpful when you are at rock bottom. Do not try to rank your trauma by comparing it to trauma you have experienced or to the experiences of others. Any therapist will tell you that pain is not comparable. If two old friends meet up on a park bench to catch up after not seeing each other for ten years and one says my wife died and I have cancer, and the other says my son died and my wife had a stroke, who is in more grief and pain? You can't compare the two situations. Each person is suffering in their own way. We cannot comprehend the situation another person is in and thus cannot compare our lives to others

11 Holmes TH, Rahe RH. The social readjustment rating scale *J. Psychosom. Res.* 1967;11:213–218.

Hitting rock bottom is always a score of one hundred on the life stress scale. Whatever your rock bottom is, you are at a one hundred. Overdosing might be one person's rock bottom, while getting a DUI could be someone else's. Both can be life-changing, serious, traumatic events. Both people are forever altered by the experience.

Your current rock bottom situation is also completely relative to your current life situation. Say you've worked your entire education to become a lawyer and have failed the bar exam. You are experiencing a massive trauma. At this moment in your life, it's the worst possible thing you can imagine. But two years later, once you've finally passed the bar on your third try and have a great job at a law firm, you may look back and realize, "Yeah, that was a really dark time for me, but I ended up getting some incredible tools that boosted my career out of studying for that damn thing three times." At the time, it was the worst-case scenario. Your life was over. But your future self sees it as the complete opposite.

If your current situation feels like a rock bottom moment, it's OK to treat it as one. But keep your future self in mind. Your brain is getting stronger. You are developing survival skills. You are going to see opportunities in life that were previously invisible to you.

Naturally, we will all hit a rock bottom several times in our lives–each rock bottom seeming like the worst. As we age, we are able to look back and pinpoint certain events that truly altered our lives. But in the moment, each rock bottom is rock bottom. My mother died on April 27, 2021. It was the greatest pain I ever felt. One year later I've written a book inspired by her life. Each individual incident is its own worst-case scenario, and each is something we must rebound from in a more powerful form. Once you climb out of that hole (and you will), you will be a changed individual, able to impact the lives of those around you in new ways and better fulfill your purpose for this whole strange journey.

## Denial is Temporary

Denial[12] is a reflex our brains use to protect us. It buys us time to process, absorb, and cope with stressful situations. It keeps us from collapsing under the weight of the trauma. Just as adrenaline numbs pain for a period of time after injury, allowing us to protect others or get to a safe place, denial allows us to continue to function until our mind is able to process the event and formulate a plan.

If you've ever lost someone you loved, you may remember simply feeling numb when it happened. For the first week, some will even continue to act as if nothing happened, going to work, answering emails, going out with friends. Research has shown that the mind even makes up stories, telling us the loved one has just gone on a trip, it's just temporary, they'll be back soon, it's just a bad dream. Denial is our brain's way of protecting us from the magnitude of the loss, allowing us to adapt more gradually. People who lose a limb often report that they can still feel their absent limb or had no sensation of the injury at all initially. Denial is an automatic, protective response that is useful in immediate crisis.

By the time you've picked up this book, though, your trauma is likely not a fresh wound. It's no longer something you can ignore. You've reached a point where you know you need to deal with it, and you cannot fathom a way out of the pain. When denial wears off, you know it is time to be brutally honest with yourself about where you're at. You open your eyes and admit just how bad the situation actually is. Rose-colored glasses are not going to help you. You must be able to examine your trauma in the cold hard light of day. See it for what it is and understand the impact it is going to have on your life. Knowledge, as always, is power.

---

12 McFarlane, A.C. (2000). On the Social Denial of Trauma and the Problem of Knowing the Past. In: Shalev, A.Y., Yehuda, R., McFarlane, A.C. (eds) International Handbook of Human Response to Trauma. Springer Series on Stress and Coping. Springer, Boston, MA.

That can be hard. And it can hurt. In the later stages of denial, you will tell yourself things aren't really all *that* bad. If you're still doing that, it's time to stop. If you have difficulty embracing the traumatic experience for what it is, it can be helpful to sit down and write out exactly what has happened and what it means. The specifics on how life has changed as you know it. Confront it. See it. Absorb it. In doing so, you will feel your survival instincts begin to emerge.

It is also at this point that you will sense your level of resilience. Understand that this book is not intended as a replacement for mental health care. If you suffer from serious clinical depression, suicidal ideation, or other debilitating mental health issues, you will need to contact outside help before moving forward. *See list of resources in the Appendix.*

Note that you should not blame yourself for where you are or beat yourself up for ending up in this situation. As humans, we all struggle with the pain that results from mistakes, bad decisions, and accidents. I am just asking that you see the situation and accept it for what it is. Because the reality of your situation fuels the drive to make change.

Those who have attended Alcoholics Anonymous will know the organization teaches that being honest with yourself and others, admitting the truth, is the crucial first step to recovery. "We admitted we were powerless over alcohol and our lives had become unmanageable."[13] Similarly, Step One to your Comeback requires being honest about your life, whether your current situation is effed up enough to scare you into action. Learn to completely embrace just how bad things are. This can be painful to do, especially if you've been able to maintain some denial. But now is the time to rip off your blinders and look your dumpster fire straight in the face. See it, feel it, breathe it, then USE it to push you up and into a new future.

---

13 Alcoholics Anonymous Big Book. 4th ed., Alcoholics Anonymous World Services, 2002.

## Remarkable Rebounds: Tim Allen

*"When I went to jail, reality hit so hard that it took my breath away, took my stance away, took my strength away."*[14]

Before Tim Allen was a famous comedian, he was a drug dealer. Allen's father died when he was 11, spiraling Allen into alcoholism and bad behavior as a teen and college student that ended when he was arrested in 1978 for dealing cocaine. He was sentenced to seven years in jail and served a little over two years. This was his rock bottom moment. He saw what prison was and did not want that for his future. Prison changed his life and his mindset. He started making other prisoners laugh. He saw that as his path forward. After his release he began working as a stand-up comic and built a career which took off with a hit network TV show (*Home Improvement*). Allen is now worth $100 million.

---

14 Fussman C. Tim Allen: What I've Learned. *Esquire.* Oct 1, 2011

CHAPTER 3

# FUEL OF CHAMPIONS

Hitting rock bottom is the critical fuel required to turn trauma into triumph, sparking an unreal level of tunnel vision focus and incessant drive. Without hitting rock bottom, or convincing your mind you've hit it, it's difficult to muster that superpower strength and the primal motivation that transforms lives into something greater than before.

## Case Study: Malik

Throughout the book, we're going to follow my client Malik so you can see the impact of the Six Steps on one person and one situation. Malik came to our firm when he was charged with a DUI years ago. Not only was he in jeopardy of license suspension and jail time, but the charge had resulted in immediate termination of his employment as a caterer. He was arrested while driving the catering van, the DUI was not his first, and he had previously been busted drinking at a work event.

Malik was the caregiver for his dad, who suffered from dementia. He needed an income to pay his rent and in-home nursing assistance for his father. Going to jail would mean his dad would have to leave their family home and move into a nursing home.

This DUI charge was Malik's rock bottom moment. When he first came to us, Malik was an "everything's gonna be fine" kind of guy. Once the denial wore off, he began to see the truth of his situation. Not only was his freedom hanging in the balance, but his dad's continued comfort and security and his own financial security were vanishing. "It's all gone to shit," he realized. "There's no way out of this."

My firm represented Malik in the DUI case, but I was determined to help him navigate the all-encompassing trauma he was facing. We spoke about the Six Steps. The first step was embracing his rock bottom moment and the power it held. Although he was on the brink of losing everything, he was also on the brink of opportunity–survival mode was kicking in. I helped him see his situation as a launching pad for building a new and better life. Malik soon realized that when you have nothing left to lose, when you're at rock bottom, there is nowhere to go but up. There is freedom in acceptance.

## Climbing Toward the Summit

That first day in court when I messed up big time, I was terrified. At that time in my life, I had no choice but to make my new Colorado law practice work–my family was depending on me. I was in such a state of emergency that it took little time to evaluate the potential consequences. I dove deep into Colorado law and learned everything there was to learn about Colorado Family Law. I worked hard at building my firm–doing the best I could for clients, making smart, sensible decisions, and being likeable. That day in court, I saw my entire career go up in flames. And those flames lit a fire under me like nothing else. If I had not hit a career bottom that day, my law firm would not have reached its full potential. We wouldn't have a reason to give our clients superior service and care. I wouldn't have been able to identify with coworkers when they experience their own adversity. My success today is directly tied to that embarrassing failure in court. It drove me to improve my skillset, to keep getting better at law.

I'm sure I would have still found a way to build a functional law firm, but I doubt it would have been as wildly successful as it is today. Why work any harder than you have to? But because I failed so spectacularly, my work ethic went into overdrive. I did everything in my power to claw myself to the top, to make up for that mistake, to repair my name. I made it to the summit of my personal mountain by falling on my ass down in the valley.

The same was true for Jaylen and Christopher. They each suffered a significant trauma in their lives, a trauma that pushed them to start from scratch and rebuild in a new direction. You may be reading this and thinking, "I can't even manage the terrible situation I am in at the moment, let alone find a way to come back from this exponentially better." There is zero sign of any bright future in the midst of trauma. We cannot see it. When I stood in that courtroom and had my ass handed to me by the Judge, the only thing I saw was my life crumbling around me. All I could hope for was getting out of that courtroom without being disbarred. It wasn't until I sat in the space of my adversity awhile that I wanted to–needed to–get up and push through.

The moment you're diagnosed with a debilitating disease is not the moment you say to the doctor, "Awesome, thanks. I'll use this to create a GoFundMe and raise enough money to cure this stupid disease." We must grieve the life we knew before the trauma, a life that is no longer, before we can look at our situation and decide not to stay in this space. That grieving process takes time, time to accept where we are, what we feel, and that we cannot return to our normal. Grieving the loss of our old life must occur before we are able to begin the climb.

## Leveraging Trauma

Do we have to suffer some great tragedy to change our lives? No. Anyone with a strong mindset and some mental toughness can make a change for the better. There are plenty of great books on that topic (some of my favorites are listed in the Suggested Reading at the back of this book). The lesson here is not about making a change to get more out of life. The lesson we are learning is how to leverage trauma to our advantage. Because with trauma, change is inevitable. The mind is going to adapt whether you like it or not. Our goal is to develop the tools necessary to ensure that adaptation is productive and beneficial, rather than debilitating. In my experience, when real adversity hits you, you don't remain the same. You either go up or go down.

It's easy to remain positive and savor the little things when your marriage is thriving, when you're healthy and fit, and when your bank accounts are in the green. But when the marriage fails, when the doctor diagnoses a terminal illness, or when your career that you worked so hard for is falling apart, that's where you must make a choice between one of two paths:

1. Use the adversity to your advantage, or
2. Let it consume you

The ability to make that choice can be learned. Six Steps, six practices, can enable you to use your trauma for good. We must recognize bad situations as a challenge, not a threat. We must recognize ourselves as warriors, not victims. As humans on this planet, we must know that inconveniences, obstacles, and full-blown brick walls come with the territory. Whatever can happen WILL happen. Expect it. Be prepared to USE it to your advantage. Adversity at any level boosts insight, focus, and drive. The more difficult the trauma, the more powerful the effect.

Those who make lemonade out of lemons do not let their trauma consume them. They see the situation for what it is–and what it can become. "Well, lookie there, life has just handed me a pile of shit again–looks like big things are just around the corner." They leverage those lemons into sweet, lucrative lemonade. Once we learn how to make lemonade out of lemons, we never forget it. It's an incredible feeling down the line, when you recognize that you have the power to steer your life in the right direction no matter what obstacles are thrown your way.

## Recognize the Pit

We know the power behind hitting rock bottom, the fuel of survival mode. But many people I speak to wonder whether their situation qualifies. After all, what is traumatic to one person may be a cakewalk for another. For those of you working on evaluating your position, here are some signs that your adversity is serious and likely to induce a major life change for better or worse.

You may have hit bottom if:

- You are experiencing adversity through a life event (divorce, injury, health scare, financial issues, arrest, etc.)
- You have lost the thing that matters most to you
- You feel there is nothing you can do to turn things around
- You feel hopeless or ashamed
- You are convinced you are a failure
- You feel disoriented and lost
- You feel terrified or panicked
- You have lost your passion for life

In other words, you are traumatized. Once the numbness of denial begins to fade, many will experience these frightening and painful feelings. You've fallen into a pit, whether you put yourself there or fate has stepped in and placed you there. Take a seat. Recognize where you are. Do not compare your trauma to other people's or to situations from your past. You're here, right now. Life is changing, and you will do more than survive. You will thrive.

## Simultaneous Valleys and Mountains

When talking about hitting rock bottom, it's important to point out that we can hit rock bottom in one area of our lives while going like gangbusters in another. Take a doctor being sued for medical malpractice. Her professional life is in distress, but she has a supportive husband, terrific friends, a charity she volunteers with that allows her to give back. She's passionate about her hobbies, she has a nice retirement account and two adoring cats. One part of her life has been blown apart, but the other parts are pretty great. This scenario does not minimize the level of trauma she is experiencing or change the fact that she is at rock bottom in her career. Yes, we are grateful for what we have, but when we are in the midst of a traumatic situation, nothing else matters.

Having a rock bottom situation in one part of your life while you are experiencing great success in others can create some cognitive dissonance. It can be hard to reconcile those two great opposites. And it is easy to allow the rock bottom situation to infect the good parts of your life. Maintaining perspective and learning to keep these areas of your life separate will help you to enjoy the good feelings while simultaneously working hard to rebound in the crisis area. Having things that are going well will only bolster your hope and strength during the rebuilding process.

It is sometimes tempting to think, well everything else is going well, so why am I fearful or angry or depressed about getting fired or divorced, or losing my mother? But adversity is not made any less painful in a positive environment. It is an obstacle, period. A massive boulder blocks your way just as much in a great mansion surrounded by a loving family as it does alone in a deep dark forest. Don't feel ashamed about feeling hopeless when other parts of your life are going well. Pain is pain, and it is the same under any circumstance.

As I mentioned earlier, my mother died last year. Throughout childhood, she taught me by example about the value of hope and growth. She raised me alone, without the help of anyone other than my grandmother and uncle, providing for us as a full-time social worker for New York State. Her passing was a life-shattering experience. My daughters, Mae and Clara, and I drove cross country following the funeral in Schenectady, NY. We brought along porcelain duck statues in honor of their grandmother. We visited Syracuse University where she went to college, drove to Hobart and William Smith Colleges where my wife Katy and I met, and took a week to see the country while telling stories about "Rah Rah" and her impact on our lives. We visited Graceland, Dollywood, and the National Civil Rights Museum. We stayed at the Peabody Hotel and the girls were Honorary Duckmasters. In this one week, my daughters helped me to pull myself up from a life blown apart.

My support system could not have been stronger. But that doesn't mean I don't struggle to this day–and likely will forever–with the pain of losing my role model and friend. Death is a life-changing obstacle. My friend, Derek Vanderwarker, told me upon losing his mom, "It's like a supernova of pain and beauty at the same time." I agree. I was able to see my pain as an opportunity. An opportunity to connect with my daughters on a once in a lifetime trip. An opportunity to reevaluate my life and what I value most. A transformational seven days was born from complete devastation. The pain of losing my hero was a bottom.

## Rock Bottom Might Creep Up on You

A lot of trauma comes from big, horrific events. Injuries, heart attacks, death, losing a job, arrests, and so on. But trauma is not always a big explosion. Sometimes it is a slow burn that sneaks up on you. My friend Kai hit rock bottom as an adult because of childhood trauma. His father was murdered when he was a young boy, and his mother was abusive, cunningly cruel, and neglectful. His siblings looked out only for their own survival.

In response to his traumatic childhood, Kai created a false self. He worked hard, obtained a scholarship, moved away from his family, and became a high-earning coder. To outsiders, he was the epitome of success. Smart, driven, perfect. He'd built a wonderful life for himself. But in Kai's own life, he struggled with a string of unsuccessful relationships. He felt unlovable and worthless. He could control his career success with hard work, but he could not control other aspects of his life. Finally, all that suppressed trauma crashed in on him. He stopped going to work. He didn't pay his bills. He didn't answer his friends' calls.

Kai hit his rock bottom when the impact of the trauma he lived through finally overtook him. His trauma had always been there, but his failure at relationships suddenly brought it to light, and it overwhelmed him. This was his deepest darkest place. I had spoken to Kai many times about the Six Steps of comebacks. He knew the drill. And once he was able to recognize his situation, he nabbed the opportunity. He found a therapist who helped him uncover suppressed memories. He confronted his mother and siblings. His crumbling life thrust him into survival mode, and he was equipped to recognize the situation and respond–coming back stronger than ever, his drive and work ethic intact, with the added bonus of learning to love and trust a partner.

Your rock bottom could be a sudden event, or it could be a slow boil that one day does you in. However you get there, rock bottom is the starting point for your comeback, your opportunity to begin building a better life than before. Remember that.

## The Rock Bottom Avalanche

For some people, the hits keep coming. You may hit rock bottom, pick yourself up, and take another hit. You're at the bottom of a well and every time someone throws you a rope, it breaks. "Maybe there's no hope for me. Maybe I'm never going to move forward. I've just got bad luck."

I'm here to tell you that's not true. You've heard the saying, "when it rains it pours," and traumatic events are no different. Most people have more than one trauma or crisis in their lives at a time. Nobody gets an easy path. I've certainly had my fair share of rock bottom avalanches. Just when I think I've got it figured out, something else happens. Life is like a used car. It overheats, you fix the radiator, and the head gasket springs a leak. It's not about you. You aren't cursed. You are most certainly not hopeless.

Whether you face an avalanche or a slow boil, the Six Steps are going to give you the tools needed to embrace every single rock-bottom moment and use each one to fuel a motivation to come back stronger. Rock bottom is not going to be your permanent address. It's a stop along the way. The more rock bottoms you hit, the stronger and better your life can become.

## Find Your Why

If you are considering building your life up better than ever using the rock bottom moment you are in now, it can help to pinpoint your "why." But in the realm of hopelessness, discovering a why isn't always easy. I can tell you that it *does* exist. You have a very important reason to rise above your current situation. If you are having difficulty identifying the "why" that is going to make you stand up and fight, there are plenty of motivations to choose from:

- Belief that your purpose is still out there
- Belief in yourself and your potential
- Love for your family
- Need to provide for your family
- Desire to give one last shot at a dream
- Wish to share your message with the world
- Determination to prove the naysayers wrong
- Drive to earn enough to fund a charity you believe in
- Interest in improving the world
- Feeling you are destined for greatness
- Refusal to accept that this is all there is

It does not matter what your reason is. But you need one. In life, our "why" is often not reachable from the path we are on. Only a major obstacle on that path can shift us in the right direction and allow us to reach our true purpose. Your future self may be able to look back and clearly see that you were on the wrong path up until that life-changing event occurred. Identifying your "why" can help you gain your footing as you prepare to navigate your way out of the pit and rise above your old life.

## Fear is Not an Option

Those who reach that point where they say, "I've HAD it. Things are going to change starting now," are in a prime position to create real and lasting change. Get upset, feel worried, anxious, nervous. Cry out loud, throw a tantrum–then start digging. We ALL have it in us. No matter your background, financial state, or family situation, you HAVE it. You just have to find that strength and that resolve.

Life isn't a drill. We get one shot. We do not fall victim to rough circumstances, threatening events, or harsh situations, because we are never hopeless. We are never powerless. We are human. We have the innate ability to push past any barrier and come out on top. Age doesn't matter. Health doesn't matter. Money doesn't matter. Every day is a chance to turn it around. Every hour. Every minute.

If anything holds us back, it's fear. But when we hit bottom, fear is obliterated. Fear is no longer an option because what we fear has now happened. Survival becomes the ONLY option. "But you don't know what I've been through. You don't know what I'm facing." It literally doesn't matter what you're facing–divorce, homelessness, imprisonment, or death. The only thing that matters is that you've hit rock bottom, which is the most opportune time to turn things around. Survival mode thrusts us into a state of focus and drive. Use it.

We are battling our mind when we hit bottom. Not our career. Not our income. Not our spouse. Not our addiction. Our mind. When we understand that adversity feeds our strength, we can conquer any obstacle. We can't predict the trials we'll have to face, how long it will take to reach the new top, what we'll have to forfeit, and we don't care. None of that matters. What matters when we hit rock bottom is that we are now headed in one direction. To the top.

From those I have worked closely with over the years, the ones who took trauma by the balls and used it to achieve their dream life, had this in common: they hit rock bottom. And not only did they hit bottom, but they recognized and embraced the power behind hitting bottom, the undying drive to produce change.

## View From Mom's Front Porch

In 2004, I was an unemployed lawyer facing a felony DUI. I sat on my mom's front porch, looking out at the grass. I was looking at her car. It was her car, her grass, and her porch of her small house in Niskayuna, NY. And I was certain I would never have a law license, let alone a house. I saw my future, and it sucked.

Alcohol was no longer my friend. It never really was. The humiliation, shame, depression, and so on was a long time coming. It was easier to change my life than it was to keep going on the way I was going. I desperately called rehab centers, and everything was more money than I had, which was zero.

To recap: I was unemployed but still had law school loans. I had no vehicle and no driver's license. I was an alcoholic. I lived in my mother's basement. This single mom, state worker, who raised a child on her own, managed to care for her son, buy multiple homes and vehicles, and helped me through every life crisis. I was living in her basement. I was embarrassed for her. Not many people remained my friend. It became evident that I never really had any friends. I had drinking buddies. I was 33. I had an inflated sense of self-worth, a massive ego, and I was afraid of most everything. And at that very moment, I was unable to hide the fact that I was ashamed of the boy I clearly was. How's that for a rock bottom?

Fast forward to today: Hitting bottom was the best thing that ever happened to me, because it was a catalyst for change, which led to more change, which led to helping other people in my sphere attack their lives. These Six Steps are based on both observation and personal experience. Believe.

## Remarkable Rebounds: Stephen Hawking

*"And however difficult life may seem, there is always something you can do and succeed at. It matters that you don't just give up."*[15]

Stephen Hawking was an up-and-coming physicist when he was diagnosed with ALS (aka Lou Gehrig's Disease) in the 1960s. His doctor told him he would lose his ability to walk, become confined to a wheelchair, lose the use of his limbs, and eventually have to rely on a voice-output communication device to speak. The average ALS patient lives four years after diagnosis.[16] Hawking lived another fifty-five years. His diagnosis was his rock bottom. And this rock bottom catapulted Hawking into one of the best-known physicists of all time. His groundbreaking research into black holes radically changed our understanding of the universe. He wrote numerous bestselling texts that are still studied by physicists worldwide. He received numerous awards, including the 2009 Presidential Medal of Freedom.

15 Hawking S. Oxford University Union lecture. November 14, 2016.

16 Alcaz S, Jarebinski M, Pekmezović T, Marinković Z, Apostolski S. Survival in amyotrophic lateral sclerosis. *Srp Arh Celok Lek.* 1997 Jan-Feb;125(1-2):19-23.

# STEP 2: EMBRACE DESPERATION

*"When one is desperate, it's not ready, aim, fire. It's ready, fire, aim."*

Desperation is usually painted as a bad thing. "He must be desperate." In reality, desperation is a powerful state. Once we hit rock bottom, desperation enters the picture, providing the driving force that makes us hunt down solutions. If we face adversity without feeling desperate, we have no incentive to find a way up and out.

Take a headline I ran across on ESPN.com recently: *Los Angeles Lakers' LeBron James, fueled by 'desperation,' drops 56 in comeback win over Warriors.*[17] James' 'desperation' moves earned him one of his highest scoring games ever, taking the Lakers from a fourteen-point deficit to an eight-point lead and the win. When asked about the incredible win, he said, "Right now, I don't give a damn about the 56. I'm just happy we got a win. That's just literally the first thing that came to my mind." James' desperation took him to the win and beyond.

Desperation is what causes us to get out of a car stuck in the snow on a lonely mountain road with no cell service and hike to the next town in a blizzard in minus fifteen degrees. Anyone stuck in that same storm with a full tank of gas, a fully charged phone, a blanket, a case of water, and a bag of granola bars, isn't desperate. They are thinking logically. They know it is dangerous to get out of the car and hike. It's safer to wait it out. But a desperate person is not limited by logic. To a desperate person, any option is

---

17 McMenamin D. Los Angeles Lakers' LeBron James, fueled by 'desperation,' drops 56 in comeback win over Warriors. *ESPN.com*. March 5, 2022.

better than the one they're in, even an illogical one. Desperation provides the superstrength necessary to visualize options that were previously invisible.

When we're desperate, we take risks. We think creatively. Desperation is the motivating force that makes us want to fight. People who pull themselves out of the worst situations of their lives do so because they are unable to accept that they are stuck. Desperation pushes us to move, to think, to search, and to take action. We come up with options that previously did not exist.

Desperation is a measure of how much we want something and what we are willing to do to get it. It's a positive energy, the beginning of change. If you feel desperate when you are in the absolute rock-bottom situation, it's a good sign. It means your body is beginning to fuel the drive and the desire it will take to get yourself out of it. Desperation forces us to move forward.

CHAPTER 4

# PULLING OUT ALL THE STOPS

Desperation is possibly the strongest motivator in the world. It is our survival instinct kicking in. Learning to embrace that desperation and let it pull you forward is key.

## Creative Exit Strategies

Renee started working for our firm a few years ago. She was engaging, enjoyable to be around, and friendly and accessible with our clients. Hiring her was a smart move on our account. We were lucky to find her.

A year ago, she shared her back story with me. Renee was an alcoholic. Her spouse had taken her kids and left. She had no job, no money, no future. She was emotionally, psychologically, and physically at her absolute rock bottom. Her kids were gone, she'd destroyed all of her relationships, and, as a stay-at-home mom, she had no work experience. And now her alcoholism was destroying her physically. That sounds bad, but wait, there's more.

Renee went to rehab. She worked hard at her recovery for months. She moved into a halfway house and continued to work towards sobriety. She started to have visits with her kids. Then her wife died. Her kids went to live with their grandmother whom Renee knew was abusive. Renee was running out of time at the halfway house and had to find a job and a place to live if she wanted to get custody of her kids back. Her case worker told her that if she didn't get a job, continue to stay sober, and move into an apartment of her own, the grandmother would get permanent guardianship.

Renee found an apartment, putting all of the money she had into the deposit. But she had to have a job to pay the rent. If she didn't find a job, she would lose her deposit, have no money to her name, and nowhere to live. Her children would be placed with their nightmare grandmother because Renee did not have a stable place to live.

Renee hit a new rock bottom. She had no money, no job, nowhere to live, and was going to lose custody of her kids. Worst-case scenario, as things stood, she didn't know if she could stay sober once everything crumbled around her. It couldn't get worse than this. She was desperate.

Renee's desperation arose from her "whys." Her kids relied on her. Her sobriety relied on her mental strength. Renee no longer controlled her mind. Desperation did. And desperation was going to find Renee a job, pay Renee's rent, block Renee from the liquor store, and bring Renee's kids home to safety. She had very little work experience and minimal education. Logic told her she could never qualify for a job that would pay enough to support herself and her kids. Desperation grabbed logic by the throat and tossed it out the window.

Looking through some job listings, Renee spotted our ad for a receptionist at Burnham Law. She had no computer skills aside from a basic internet search and some social media, no experience. Going back to school was out of the question. There was no time. She–or rather her desperation–read the job description, the tasks she would need to be able to perform. She Googled how to perform those tasks. Trained herself on the computer skills listed by watching YouTube videos and practicing. She Googled how a professional receptionist should act. Desperation told her, *fake it till you make it.*

Renee Googled examples of receptionist resumes, noted the format and structure, and put together her new resume–a tiny experience and education section, but a large section listing her new skills and abilities. She found an interview outfit at a secondhand store. She was on autopilot, throwing everything she had at this one shot. It was sink or swim. Desperation was in control, morphing an impossibility into reality.

She came in for the interview. Our staff adored her. She was a star. We hired her immediately. Renee was thrilled and grateful for the opportunity to be able to keep that apartment, earn an income, get her kids back, and stay sober. In Renee, we scored a goldmine. We were thrilled to have found such an intelligent, engaging, and professional individual. It was a win-win situation for everyone.

Renee's desperation was what got her out of her rock bottom. Her desperation pushed her to find a way out. It was a strong, driving force that got her on her feet and forced her to take action. She found a solution and went after it. She was so desperate that her certainty that she was unqualified could not get in her way.

Many of us want better things for our lives. More money, a better home, a better marriage. But without desperation, it's easier to settle for what we have. This is yet another silver lining to the traumatic situations we go through in life. Yes, things may seem impossible now. But desperation is going to kick in and open up doors you had no idea existed. Renee's desperate state allowed her to identify what she wanted and make it happen–even when it seemed completely impossible.

## Desperate Times Call for Desperate Measures

Depression is a lack of energy and motivation. Desperation, in contrast, is all about energy and motivation. It is a force that either pushes or literally drags you forward to do something, *anything*. It's hard to understand desperation until you've felt it. A desperate person doesn't look for solutions. They pound the walls, pry at the hinges on the door, and jump up to scrape the ceiling, over and over, looking for a way out. They try everything.

Desperation is a survival instinct. Our early ancestors experienced a lot of desperation, living in caves and surviving only on what they could kill or find to eat. You can be certain it was desperation that drove those early people to figure out how they could band together as hunters to kill a giant woolly mammoth. Only completely desperate people would attempt to do something that crazy. If those same ancestors of ours were sitting down to three square meals a day every day, there's no way they ever would have contemplated hunting the mammoth. But they were hungry. Their kids were hungry. They had to eat. They needed to survive. Desperation provided the crazy scheme of working together to kill a mammoth, supplying food for weeks. It took a lot of tries and a lot of planning to discover what worked. Their desperation forced them to come up with brand new ideas.

## Why Desperation Works

Desperation has two important components: (1) It forces us to take action and (2) it forces us to be creative. Those two things together are what make desperation such a powerful tool. If we take action without being creative, it's not as effective. And if we are creative without an overwhelming driving force, it won't get us anywhere. The two components together are the special sauce that allows desperation to pull us out of adversity.

Renee could have been creative and spent hours brainstorming jobs she could do, skills she could learn, or solutions. Being creative is great, but unless you tie it to action, it gets you nowhere. It was only when Renee was creative AND took action that she was able to move herself forward out of trauma. Let your desperation lead you. Let it take over. Follow wherever it leads you. It will get you out of adversity. It's not a plan of action. It's just action. When one is desperate, it's not ready, aim, fire. It's ready, fire, aim.

## Remarkable Rebounds: Stephen King

*"Sometimes you have to go on when you don't feel like it, and sometimes you're doing good work when it feels like all you're managing is to shovel shit from a sitting position."*[18]

Stephen King grew up in poverty after his father walked out on the family. He developed intense emotional distress as a child. He began using alcohol and drugs but graduated from college. He couldn't find a job and had to work in a laundromat, writing at night and on weekends. He eventually got a job teaching but had to keep the laundry job to make ends meet. He kept writing in his spare time and after many rejections, he sold his first novel. But drugs and alcohol were an integral part of his writing process. He feared that without them he would lose his ability to write at all and simply could not stop using. His addictions grew worse and worse. In the 1980s, his wife finally gave him an ultimatum about getting clean. He was able to quit, but his worst fear came true: he was unable to write at all once he was sober. This was his rock bottom. His wife helped him begin to write one word after another. His writing had new depth and insight. He came back a stronger, more influential writer than ever before. King has published 61 books and sold more than 350 million copies. His net worth is more than $500 million.

---

18 King S. *On Writing: A Memoir of the Craft.* Simon and Schuster, 2000.

CHAPTER 5

# DESPERATION IS ROCKET FUEL

The thing about desperation is that it doesn't allow for planning. You don't have time to sit back, assess your choices, consider options, or compare them. There is no studying or researching. You have no time for preparation or planning. You don't have the option of being thoughtful, precise, or careful.

Desperation prompts immediate action. You do not have time to think things through and try to find logical solutions. If we waited to aim before firing in a high-stakes situation, chances are we wouldn't get past aim. 'Ready, Aim, Fire' sounds great, and for some people it works, but it has never worked for me. I get caught up in the details, in the unknown, and end up wasting a lot of valuable time and energy without any payoff.

Desperation allows us to DO first, think later. Take action, then evaluate the results. Aiming after firing allows us to consider the data that we have generated over however many months and, armed with accurate data and experience, we are better able to alter our charted course. Slight adjustments can happen once you are full steam ahead, and this is more effective than spending hours sweating the details of some hypothetical plan.

Once you've taken action and are ready to evaluate the results, you'll need to use your mistakes and failures to grow. Now you can aim. And when you do, remember what technical advisor Mark Baker told Mel Gibson and Heath Ledger when teaching them how to shoot a muzzle-loading rifle. "Aim small, miss small." When you aim at a man and miss, you miss the man. If you aim at a button on the man's jacket and miss, you still hit the man. Instead of aiming to buy a home, aim to save $500 a week. Instead of aiming for a promotion, aim for a compliment on your current project. In addition to evaluating the mistakes and failures of your action, targeting small, specific goals will minimize the odds of making further mistakes.

## Inspiration vs. Desperation

A lot of self-help books talk about inspiration. They encourage people to make vision boards, create ten-year goals and listen to TED Talks that will inspire them. Look, I'm not going to knock inspiration. Wanting what others have is certainly a powerful force. Everyone I know, including me, has role models, people we look up to, those that motivate us to be more successful in our lives. But again, this book isn't about wanting to make a change. It's about *needing* to. When we are facing incredible adversity, we aren't going to feel inspired by anything. We feel like there is no way out, no way up. The compelling force of Inspiration is lost in times of trauma. Inspiration is light and airy, a powerful magician that floats in to help guide us when all is well with the world. Desperation is a down-and-dirty warrior who kicks down the door to save us when our world is falling apart.

Those same self-help books will tell you that desperation is a weakened state, that we should not allow ourselves to get to that point. I'm here to tell you that's backwards. Through centuries of human development, our brains have refined the state of desperation as a tool for survival. Pretending things are fine to appear strong and in control is just that–pretend. The anxiety and stress that we feel when our situation becomes desperate pushes us to take actions we never would have imagined possible. Embrace them.

Inspiration implies you have time to daydream, read a book, cut out pictures from *Luxury Home* magazine while sipping a latte. Desperation is robbing a bank. Desperation is inspiration's feral cousin. Desperation means you must do something right now, and you will throw absolutely anything at the wall to see if it sticks. In this state, your mind is able to come up with crazy schemes. Things are so bad that even the most ridiculous ideas have just as many odds of working as any well-thought-out plan. If you feel desperate about the situation you have found yourself in, you are not weak. You have not failed. You are empowered to take on this situation with a drive and creativity that is beyond anything you can imagine.

## Desperation Evaporates Paralysis

Change is uncomfortable. When we think about making a change, whether big or small, it's not uncommon to become overwhelmed with what-ifs. That's the benefit of hitting bottom. Without the bottom, and the accompanying desperation, the analysis was academic. When I hit rock bottom, I knew I had to make a change to get out of the situation, but then I started thinking about what that change might look like. I made lists. I considered options. I weighed the pros and cons. And I became paralyzed, unable to think about my situation at all. I turned away. Refused to address it. That list of pros and cons can be a killer. To the human brain, one con is enough to dissuade us from change, no matter how many pros we can muster up. It's not rabid. Desperation is rabid.

It's called 'analysis paralysis.' Our mind rolls ideas over and over, looking for new information and new arguments. Eventually, we become so afraid that we'll make the wrong decision, we end up making no decision at all. What if I pick the wrong option? What if there are other choices I didn't consider? You could pave a road to the horizon with what-ifs.

But when we are in a desperate enough situation, we don't have time to go over all of the what-ifs. There are very few options available anyhow. Even if we do have some choices, we do not have time to do an in-depth analysis. We're in a spot where we must do something now.

Desperation obliterates analysis paralysis. It motivates us to move forward with something, anything! Anything other than the rock bottom situation we've found ourselves in is a good step at this point. Desperation motivates us to push ahead even though we don't have all the facts, options, or any idea of how to navigate the options that seem feasible.

In a desperate state, we are free to push through. The what-ifs no longer matter. Analysis goes out the window. Plotting, planning, evaluating, and scrutinizing are no longer needed. All you're left with are your instincts and creativity. Follow them. They will not let you down. The more you embrace this moment of desperation and the power if offers, the stronger you get.

## Creativity Breeds Options

The more desperate you become, the more creative you become. New, off-the-wall options start to materialize. In a recent Carolina Panthers football game, the place kicker was injured in the pre-game warm-up. The team did not have another player who would kick field goals. For all the fourth downs, regardless of the distance needed to get the down, they had to go for it. This has never happened before in NFL football.

They had no option to kick a field goal during the game, a major strategy used by teams to win. This was a desperate situation. There was no back-up plan. The coaches had to make the decision right then and there that they could not attempt a single field goal. They had to go for two-point conversions after every touchdown. This desperate situation changed their entire approach to the game, forcing them to be creative and come up with solutions they had no time to analyze or weigh. Fire, then aim. They lost the game but discovered a powerful new tool: how to work without a place kicker. Desperation is the reason we continue to set records, to grow. Without it, we would never reach the levels of creativity required to advance.

Desperation has also led to untrained people being put in as NHL goalies. When the starter and the back-up goalie are suddenly injured or ill, and there's no time to call someone up from a minor league, teams have put in equipment managers, relatives of players, bankers in the community, grad students, and web producers to man the net–and won the game. A ridiculous concept when you think about it. But in times of desperation, we don't think about it.

If you've ever been home alone with a toddler when the power goes out (no screens!), it's too cold to play outside, and your car won't start, you have known desperation. You find crazy creative ways to keep your kid busy and occupied, things you would never consider on a regular day. Sometimes the games you invent on those days become long-standing favorites. If you've ever been in the middle of making dinner and realize you are missing a key ingredient and don't have time to go to the store, your desperation pushes you to find a substitute. Women on the home front dealing with food shortages during World War II concocted many popular recipes still in use today, out of desperation. My grandmother's signature chocolate cake recipe calls for Miracle Whip instead of oil and eggs. Necessity is the mother of invention.

## Desperation Kills Procrastination

Desperation forces us to move and to move immediately. When we are at a rock-bottom point in our life, procrastination becomes less attractive. We may want to procrastinate on some massive, daunting new work project. I'll start tomorrow. What's 24 hours? But when the boss bursts in and tells us we have one day to finish the assignment or we're out on our ass, we'd rather do the work now and save procrastination for later.

Juan, another client of ours, recently lost his job. A huge hit to his self-esteem. He was an educated, professional guy who had recently overcome cancer and was putting the financial pieces of his life back together. After using most of his money to pay for the out-of-network treatment he needed, he thought things were on the upswing. This job was his path to a comfortable and successful future. But he found himself being escorted to the door the day his company was bought. He came home with his box of pens and photos and coffee mugs and sat on the couch for two months playing video games. He couldn't face a job search. He put it off.

He went for a routine follow-up exam. The cancer was back. Now Juan absolutely had to get a job with insurance so he could get the ongoing care he needed to beat that cancer and pay his bills. He was suddenly desperate. Procrastination was no longer an option. Juan got on the computer that night, updated his resume, scrolled LinkedIn and Indeed, and applied for 20 jobs. He was hired within a week. His desperation forced him to get up and take action. What could have taken years (it takes a long time to find a job playing video games) took one week. He's got a job that is better than the last one and he's cancer-free. The moment he lost his job, his future looked so bleak that he could not move to change it. But if things get bad enough, desperation will drive us to push forward and find solutions.

Imagine putting yourself in an escape room. You're stuck, locked in, and if you want to win the game, you have to use every brain cell, pull on all your strength, all your courage, try everything possible. In an escape room you have limited resources, a lot of roadblocks, and a ticking timer. A rock-bottom scenario coupled with desperation creates the same atmosphere. You're locked in, the clock is ticking, it's time to think outside the box.

When we're desperate, we don't need a game plan. We don't need a roadmap. We don't even have to know where the heck we're going. What we need is the strength and creativity to find just one thing that works. One. Then and only then do we think about the next step. And then the next.

## Burn the Ships

The phrase "Burn the Ships" was derived from a not entirely accurate, yet popular story.[19] In 1519, Spanish Conquistador Hernando Cortés landed on the shores of the Yucatan in Mexico with one objective: to seize the great treasures the Aztecs had hoarded there. The mission wouldn't be an easy one, but Cortés was a powerful influencer. As the story goes, he was able to persuade over 100 sailors and 500 soldiers to board eleven ships in Spain and set out for Mexico, promising them riches to last for generations.

People at the time were baffled at how a small band of Spanish soldiers were able to arrive in a strange country and swiftly overthrow a large empire that had been in power for over six centuries. For Cortés, the answer was easy. It was all or nothing. A complete and total commitment. Cortés got the buy-in from the rest of his men by taking away the option of failure. It was conquer and be heroes and enjoy the spoils of victory. . . or DIE! When Cortés and his men arrived at their destination, he pumped them up for the ensuing battle with three words. "Burn the ships!"

The men erupted in resistance. Destroy their only ride home? They were surrounded by some of the most dangerous warriors on Earth. And he's asking them to eliminate their only means of escape? Cortés repeated his

---

19 Reynolds WA. The Burning Ships of Hernán Cortés. *Hispania.* Vol. 42, No. 3 (Sep. 1959), pp. 317-324.

command. "Burn the ships!" adding, "If we are going home, we are going home in their ships."[20] The men did as their leader asked and destroyed the 11 ships they had arrived in. This changed everything. The men went from wanting to win the battle to *needing* to win the battle. Cortés had instilled desperation.

Incredibly, the men conquered the Aztecs. While I am certainly not endorsing the horrific, destructive, and violent acts of the Spanish, I cannot help but use this tale to emphasize how desperation allowed these men to succeed where others had been unsuccessful for six centuries. They had no other option. No escape. No fallback position. It was succeed or die. Desperation is a major force in producing change. The desperate person is anything but weak.

## Pitfalls to Avoid

Now that you see the value of desperation, I need to caution you not to let desperation overtake your moral compass or your rational mind. Useful, productive desperation will never push you to the point of breaking the law, harming someone, or endangering your health. Those are not solutions. They are mistakes. I want you to embrace your desperation as a tool to dig yourself out of the hole, not further in. To discover creative, productive, helpful options, and opportunities that will propel you forward out of your situation.

While desperation eliminates analysis paralysis, kills procrastination, and breeds creativity and action, it does not override good sense. Desperation pushes us to act now, but in that action, we must remain human, we must

20 The truth of this story is 10 of 11 ships were destroyed, not burned, but this has become a popular story most people are familiar with [Smith KN. Searching for the ships Cortes burned before destroying the Aztecs. *ARS Technica.* Feb. 28, 2019].

stay in touch with reality and recognize that our actions have consequences. They can harm others or take us further into despair. Remember, your desperation should drive you to productive, forward-reaching actions and solutions. If there is nothing positive in the action, it's not going to help you.

This is not to say that your desperation can't drive you to do risky things. The whole point of desperation is that it pushes you against the wall so that you're ready to do things you never would have imagined. For one person, that might mean hanging out in a building's lobby to force some face time with the CEO by whom they want to be hired. For someone else, it might mean selling roses on a street corner to get the cash to pay for a van they can live in. It could mean packing up and moving across the country, without a job or a plan, to maintain a consistent presence in your kids' lives after a divorce.

There is no fear of failure when things are desperate. They cannot get worse. Anything you try gives you a chance of improving things, as long as it does not harm you or others. A 10-percent chance that your seat-of-the-pants Hail Mary pass will save you is 10 percent better than the 100 percent chance you will remain at rock bottom if you do nothing.

## Remarkable Rebounds: Marc Zupan

*"My injury has led me to opportunities and experiences and friendships I would never have had before. And it has taught me about myself. In some ways, it's the best thing that ever happened to me."*[21]

Marc Zupan was just a regular college kid when he got drunk and fell asleep in the back of a friend's truck. The friend drove away, not knowing he was back there, and he was thrown from the truck and suffered injuries that left him quadriplegic. This was his rock-bottom moment. Zupan healed and got his college degree and became a national champion in quad rugby twice, also being named player of the year. He went on to win a bronze medal and a gold medal on the U.S. Paralympics team. He has appeared in many TV shows and movies and wrote an autobiography. He works full-time as a civil engineer.

---

21 Rubin, H. A., & Shapiro, D. A. (2005). Murderball. MTV Films.

## CHAPTER 6

# LET DESPERATION BE YOUR NORTH STAR

Our receptionist Renee didn't have a well-thought-out plan for her life. She didn't have a 10-year plan, a five-year plan, or even a one-month plan. It was all she could do to get sober and survive. She needed a job, any job, and she needed it ASAP. There was no plan.

Fast forward two years. Renee is now in a leadership role, owns a home where she lives with her kids. She has full custody. She is two and a half years sober. She took a chance out of desperation, and it paid off. Renee is where she is because she recognized she had hit rock bottom and did not fight the creativity and drive that comes with desperation. She has achieved success she could never have imagined when she was broke, drinking, and facing the loss of her children.

### Case Study: Malik

Remember in Step 1, I introduced you to Malik, my DUI client who had lost his job, was facing prison, and had to place his dad in a nursing home. Malik accepted he'd hit rock bottom. I helped him leverage his desperation. Malik was sentenced to 30 days in jail, a light sentence, but still 30 days he would be unable to earn an income and take care of his dad.

Malik was desperate to find a solution, and in his desperation, he got wildly creative. He tried everything until he came up with one spectacular idea. Malik applied for respite caregiver help through a state program. This gave him some care for his dad, but not enough. So, Malik leveraged his family and neighborhood, whipping up a schedule of folks to bring meals and come in every few hours to spend time with his dad. His younger cousin moved in for a month and was able to spend the nights there (this helped the cousin save money for truck driving school). Malik used every resource and idea he had and found a solution. He was able to keep his dad at home until he was released from jail. Without desperation, Malik would never have had the creative drive to detect the options that ended up working so well for him and his family.

Malik's care for his dad was his "why," the driving force, but his own life benefitted from the hardship as well. He realized he had been drinking heavily, partly due to feeling stunted in his job. He loved the food business, but he wanted more. He wanted to attend culinary school. While waiting for his trial, Malik researched schools and found a program he'd like to try once he completed his sentence. A complete rock-bottom moment in his career forced him to reconsider what he wanted out of life. He was able to visualize a new path forward that he'd never felt there was time for in the past.

## Create Desperation

We know that when you recognize you've hit rock bottom, that desperation can create change to move yourself forward. But you don't have to be in a desperate situation to create this kind of extreme change in your life. You can mind-hack yourself into being desperate at any point in your life. Like Plato says, necessity is the mother of invention.

Convincing yourself that you have to act immediately to accomplish a goal or to get a positive outcome will help you reach a desperate, creative, driven mindset. Psych yourself into *needing* rather than wanting your goal. Create some panic in your soul. Tell yourself there's no time for planning and thinking. You have to act NOW. Your entire way of life depends on reaching this one goal. The building is burning, and you must take your next step right this second. If you can convince yourself that your survival depends on you jumping in and trying something, anything, you will discover reserves of strength and creativity you didn't know you had.

## Desperation Makes You Stronger

Whether the desperation arises from hitting rock bottom or you mind hack your way into it, you will be shocked at the power of these rarely used mental muscles. And the more you use them, the stronger they become. Your mind will learn to stop procrastinating, and you will have more creativity at your disposal for use in all aspects of your life.

You may have seen or heard about the 80s movie *Big*, starring Tom Hanks. David Moscow was the child actor cast as Hanks' character's childhood best friend. Moscow did not go on to become a big star. Instead, like many child actors, he struggled to find his way. In a recent interview he said, "I think failing might be the best gift that I was given as a child actor—not the moments where I was successful, because that's kind of easy."[22] The adversity he faced when trying to build a career–and failing–made him stronger and more creative. He eventually went on to co-develop and co-produce Lin Manuel-Miranda's *In the Heights*. Because he did not have an easy path forward, he was able to realize his true talent and place in a brand-new path.

---

22 Lilburn A, Artavia D. 'Big' star David Moscow says 'failing might be the best gift that I was given as a child actor' *Yahoo Entertainment*. December 12, 2021.

## Leverage Desperation

No one would wish desperation on themselves or others. Rock bottom is traumatizing, stressful, and terrifying. We feel hopeless and exhausted. But we all end up there at some point. While we are there, we must harness the energy of those feelings swirling around us. There is energy in ALL emotions. Make that energy work for you.

Harnessing desperation is similar to the concept of "don't get mad, get even." Instead of being carried by the swell of anger, we can use the extreme power behind that anger to constructively seek revenge in the form of productivity and success. Utilizing desperation is the same exact concept. Coalesce the energy that is created by your emotional response to your situation and use it as a driving force to take action.

If it helps, let yourself feel anger towards your situation. Be angry at the heart disease that landed you in the hospital. Be mad at the boyfriend who cleaned out your bank account and disappeared. Use that anger to make progress. Throw yourself into a memoir or blog that helps others in your situation. Create a bigger bank account with a new career. Use the energy of desperation to find solutions and possibilities you wouldn't see otherwise.

## Manifest Solutions

There's a lot of self-help stuff about manifesting. Ask and the universe will provide. I am familiar with many of these books and do believe in the universal law of attraction. But the universe isn't going to hand you a way out of your current situation. It doesn't work that way. If you believe that, you'll be left sitting in your rock bottom with no way out. The way manifestation works is by deciding you need a change, positioning yourself to see it, and jumping on any and every opportunity. You can't see something if your eyes are not open. You can't come up with solutions if you don't activate your brain to move in that direction. Visualize the life you dream of, and the answers will seem to magically appear. But, in actuality, they've always been there. It's only when you look for them and put yourself in a position to find them that you are able to access them. The law of attraction relies heavily upon the positive messaging that must be present.

The universe did not hand Renee the job at our office. She dug through job ads telling herself, "I AM going to get a job." She saw our ad because she was looking for it. The ad didn't jump out of the paper and bite her. She positioned herself to receive the solution. That's how you manifest pathways out of trauma. You tell yourself you can't wait to be out of the pit. You visualize how nice it will be. You program your brain to be on the alert. It will scan for options, and you will begin to recognize potential solutions that pass in front of you. You have to push the start button.

## Grasp at Straws

During moments of desperation, we don't have the time to do research and consider 40 different options. We are going to blindly flail around and try whatever presents itself. And a lot of things we try might not work. That's OK, because one thing will. And in the process, we will learn how to make quality-paced decisions, recognizing when something isn't working, and teaching ourselves to improve our pivot times. Remember, it's ready, fire, aim. Don't look for the perfect solution. Try a solution, keep the attention focused on the solution, and make a change when necessary. These are important failures–they are teachers.

In desperation, you're going to throw a lot of stuff at the wall. Fill your hands with stuff and chuck it. Something will stick, and that will be your path moving forward. Renee sifted through a lot of job ads. Our job happened to be the one that was a perfect fit for her. But it was never something she could have imagined herself doing. She only saw the job because she was looking for anything that would pay what she needed. She had no idea that she could actually land the job. In fact, she was pretty sure she wouldn't. But she tried anyhow. She threw it at the wall, and it stuck. She tried everything and one thing worked.

## Ignore Failure

Embracing desperation also means forgetting that failure exists. At this point, your whole life is feeling like a failure, right? At least that's the story you're telling yourself. That's the status quo, so there's nothing to be afraid of. You're living your rock bottom. If you try something and it doesn't work, it can't possibly make things worse. If you try 10 options and one works, you won't remember nine that didn't. So don't think of them as failures now. They are simply part of the package of options that is going to move you forward. They aren't failures. They are lessons. There's no time for judgment in times of desperation. Don't evaluate. Just try things. Be ready to move. Every single thing is worth a try, because each one might be your way out. It is the sheer number of tries that is going to result in your one success. If you don't try for all of them, you're not going to find the one that works.

Thomas Edison invented the incandescent electric light bulb, but nothing about this groundbreaking invention was an instant success. It was a process of trying, failing, learning from the failures, and trying again with the newfound knowledge. It took him over 10,000 little adjustments and experiments to come up with a filament that held a light. When asked what Edison felt about failing 10,000 times, his long-time associate Walter

Mallory said, "If it fails on its merits, he doesn't worry or fret about it, but, on the contrary, regards it as a useful fact learned; remains cheerful and tries something else. I have known him to reverse an unsuccessful experiment and come out all right."[23] The things you have tried and are trying are all pieces of one process: your comeback. Each piece is a success because you have tried it.

Each small failure is another step forward. The failures lead you to the successes. Finding your path forward out of trauma is about trial and error. Failure is progress. Failure is also action. And action is what will move you forward. Just stick with it. Keep trying things. Keep moving. Don't stop.

"Every adversity, every failure, every heartbreak, carries with it the seed of an equal or greater benefit." – Napoleon Hill

If you look at the options you try and say, "Well, I failed at that one, and that one, and that one," you are going to be embrace fear, not desperation. Fear paralyzes us. Desperation ensures that we must move forward. Failure and desperation breed strength and power. The dark days and hard times you experience are not wasted. They are powerful building blocks of resilience, creativity, and courage. Embrace the desperation you experience when your world falls apart. Welcome it. Let it overtake you. Invite it to stay.

---

23 Dyer FL, Martin DC. (1910). *Edison: His Life and Inventions.* Harper & Brothers, New York.

## Remarkable Rebounds: Dolly Parton

*"You just have to pray, if you're a faith-based person, for strength. If not, you just have to keep your wits about you and lean on your higher wisdom to know that things happen, and most things we get through, and usually, we come out better on the other side."*[24]

Dolly Parton grew up as one of 12 children on a farm deep in the Appalachian Mountains in a two-room cabin with no running water or electricity. Her father, a poor sharecropper, paid the doctor who delivered her with a bag of grain. Many people know her song "Coat of Many Colors," which tells the true story of how her mother sewed her a coat from scraps and how she was mocked at school for wearing it. This moment could be seen as a rock bottom for young Dolly. But she kept moving forward. As a child she was always singing and performing. Her uncle gave her a guitar and got her on the radio, starting her career. She moved to Nashville the day after her high school graduation. Parton worked incredibly hard for many years before becoming the cultural icon she is today. She has written more than 3000 songs, 25 of which were number one hits, including the massive Whitney Houston hit "I Will Always Love You" and owns Dollywood amusement park. Her Imagination Library has gifted over 172 million books to children. She helped fund a Covid vaccine and then declined to have a statue erected in her honor for it. I brought Mae and Clara to Dollywood to have fun obviously, but also to introduce them to a strong female role model who shared values similar to their grandmother's.

---

24 Carroll N. Dolly Parton: 'The whole magic about me is that I look artificial, but I'm totally real.' *USA Today.* Aug. 27, 2020.

## From Front Porch to Front Steps

The thought of never drinking alcohol again crossed my mind many times over the years. It wasn't until I hit rock bottom that I believed it was possible. Sitting on mom's front porch, realizing at that moment that my life sucked and the prospect of a bright future was non-existent.

I knew I needed to stop drinking and, finally, I was desperate. I called every rehab center in the area. I didn't have a job and therefore I didn't have insurance. "Hi. I'm Todd. I desperately want to stop drinking. I don't have any money, but I promise to pay when I can." I was asking for someone to give me the gift of life without anything in return. I begged. I promised the world. I was the squeaky wheel. I had attended a 12-Step meeting here and there, but I knew I needed inpatient rehab. I had no track record for success. I just couldn't and wouldn't quit.

Finally, after failing to find a solution–the solution–for days, I eventually found someone at a local inpatient facility who helped me apply for a scholarship. I was accepted! I agreed to do whatever they told me to do. As my mom and Aunt Sharon dropped me off, I remember thinking, this is my lowest point but I'm not totally alone (Thank you Mom and Sharon). I had some hope, and I just caught a break. Looking back, my desperation fueled my actions. I was getting into rehab come hell or high water. I didn't care what people said about me; I didn't care about anything other than saving my life.

# STEP 3: GET YOUR MIND RIGHT

*"Even five minutes of meditation per day total is enough to create significant change in thought patterns and performance."*

The phrase "get your mind right" is a tad harsh, right? I mean, the last thing those of us who've just lost a loved one want to hear is, "get your mind right." How is one supposed to get their mind right when their children are at risk of being taken from them? Did anyone tell Christopher Reeves to "get your mind right" when he came out of his riding accident a quadriplegic? Is it even remotely appropriate to tell someone going through trauma that they need to get their mind right?

It might help to define what I mean by "get your mind right." In identifying the six common traits of people who come out of severe adversity greater than before, the third trait they all possessed was a positive mental state. And while some of them had this positive mental state before hitting rock bottom and becoming desperate, many were not what I would call "positive thinkers" until after. In other words, getting your mind right can be taught, and it is never too late (or too early) to start. Any time is the right time to learn lemonade-making.

Those who came out of traumatic situations with an improved quality of life all (1) knew they'd hit rock bottom, (2) were desperate to change, and (3) rallied their thought process (got their mind right). By step 3, we've hit the proverbial fork in the road. Will we go backward from here, or forward? Negative or positive? Those who select the positive road are invariably the ones who come out on top. If all you think is how much something sucks, you will soon find that most things suck. Fact.

We've all heard the advice, "Just think positive!" or "Focus on the good things!" But that's not at all what I mean here. Getting your mind right is not a distraction from your current situation. It is not a denial of your current situation. Rather, it's the opposite. Getting your mind right requires you to embrace the place you are in and actively use it to change the way your mind is working. It takes action. It takes intention. It takes practice. Like anything, the more times you do something the better you get at it.

You're in the lemonade business now. You aren't out shopping for cocoa or coffee beans to make your lemonade. You've got lemons. And you're prepared to use them to earn that coin. You are now the freaking CEO of lemonade. You have a choice as to whether you will view adversity/trauma in your life as positive or negative. Make the choice, pick your direction, and move forward with that mindset. Getting your mind right doesn't eliminate pain. Rainbows and unicorns aren't going to suddenly breeze into your pit of despair. It is simply an action. A step. A decision.

Directing your mind to take the positive path over the negative is certainly easier for those who have practiced the skill ahead of time. But like I said, anyone at *any* point in their lives can learn to do it, as long as they have the right tools. Add these tools to your daily routine and you'll have it down.

CHAPTER 7

# OVERPOWERING NEGATIVE ENERGY

Of course, in response to trauma, the negative path is inviting. We are human. When our lives are turned on their axis, it seems almost comforting to give up, to stop caring about what the hell happens in the end, to accept the best is over. It somehow feels nice to blame ourselves for the tragedy raining down around us. *If only I'd bought that house in the valley, my home wouldn't have been struck by lightning and burned to the ground.* Blaming ourselves is a mechanism our brain uses to make sense of it all, to give us a sense of control over the chaos. Negative thinking covers us like a cozy blanket in times of severe adversity. And just like alcohol, overeating, heroin, gambling, it renders us incapacitated.

## Negativity Thwarts Opportunity

When I began my career in Colorado, I was dealing with a lot of stress and many challenges. I had just moved to a new state and was trying to build my law practice. I was trying to provide for my family financially. Emotionally, I was working on building relationships with my two stepchildren and ensuring my marriage remained happy and healthy. A lot of pressure. Those were some huge mountains I had to climb. I was under tremendous stress. Every move was sink or swim. If I dropped one ball, the entire thing was going to collapse. I would become a professional and personal failure. And all of this was going on during the 2009 recession.

My wife and I were married in July 2009. At the time, I was trying to keep my New York based title company off of life support. I was in the real estate business in New York. As the recession dragged on, little by little, the title company faded. We were left with one bank as a client. And by "one bank," I mean I had every single egg in one basket. Most banks weren't lending or were out of business. This was the only source of income for my new family. Katy's retail maternity business was shut down. Our home was in foreclosure. This one bank was my only remaining client, all of our business with the one bank, and the president of this bank was not very professional or kind in my opinion.

Three hours before my July 10 wedding, I received a call from the bank's president. I answered to him screaming at the top of his lungs that I sucked, my law firm and title company sucked, that we were too slow, and he was done with us. I had this man's rage in my head at a time that I should have been focused on my wife and our future. And this guy just tossed our future overboard. I tried to schedule a day-after breakfast, but it was too late. I was overcome with fear. I was about to be a stepfather, our house was in foreclosure, and my only source of income just told me that he was outta there. At this fork in the road, overwhelming fear lured me down the negative path.

I embraced a negative mindset. Work was hard, family was hard, everything was hard. For years I grinded. I was focused on survival. I wasn't feeling great about myself. The profound stress started affecting me physically. I developed peripheral neuropathy in my fingers and my legs. I couldn't jog. I was starting to have falls. A neurosurgeon told me I had all the symptoms of multiple sclerosis (MS). She scheduled me for a brain X-ray. If it revealed an image that looked like a lit Christmas tree, then I had multiple sclerosis.

I was a complete mess for days waiting for that scheduled test. I wasn't focused at work. I was distracted at home. I lost precious days of my life to darkness. I knew if that MRI came back lit up like a Christmas tree, it was MS. If it didn't, I wouldn't know what I had, but I would know it wasn't MS. I spent 40 minutes sobbing in the waiting room. My life was shit. It's all over. With MS, I wouldn't be able to build my law practice and support my new family. I was going to let everyone down. My life was not going to be what I'd hoped. All the negative consequences flashed before my eyes as I waited to receive my devastating diagnosis (which I'd convinced myself was MS).

The results came back negative for MS. The doctor diagnosed me with Guillain-Barré syndrome, treatable through simple immunoglobulin therapy. Another two weeks, and I would've died. I'm convinced that the stress caused Guillain-Barré.

My health returned rapidly with treatment, but I will never forget those 40 minutes I wallowed in that ER waiting room. My immediate response to adversity was appalling. I bolted off down the negative path, full sprint. My mindset was 100 percent negative. I didn't consider any other outcome than MS. My reaction was debilitating, destructive, powerless, hopeless, pointless, ineffective, and unproductive. It was not only a waste of energy, but a depletion of energy. I wasted all that energy and time trying to force my mind to accept the negative outcome.

Why hadn't I sat there and mapped out a plan for moving forward with MS? Why hadn't my mind started churning with exciting ideas for a new career path that would accommodate my impending diagnosis? A brand-new way of life? Better yet, why hadn't my mind started flashing visions of the piñata I was going to smash to celebrate a negative MS test? Why wasn't I envisioning the beauty and wonder that is my life? Instead, I fled down the negative path, where my entire life was crap and nothing good would ever come to me, without looking back.

This was a crossroads, and I'd wasted 40 minutes and countless hours running down the wrong path. If you are doing the same, stop now. Take a breath, haul your ass back to the fork in the road, and take the positive route. It is never too late. If you are on a positive path now, make a point to stay there no matter what happens around you.

When we adjust our mindset to positive, not only do we save valuable time and energy, but we open our eyes to opportunity. We become blind to opportunity on the negative road, unable to see anything but darkness. On the positive road in the midst of trauma, things are dark, yes. But we have a brilliant flashlight that bounces off the amazing landscape surrounding us.

I still think of that bank president often. I'm convinced that the pressure I was putting myself under once I moved to Colorado finally took me out. For years afterwards, I envisioned falling into an abyss and taking my wife and two stepsons with me. I became physically unable to cope. My body was giving out. I stopped working out. I ate poorly, usually subsisting on gas station donuts and coffee. I gained 35 pounds. My body ached. I didn't yet possess the warrior spirit. Only years later, after identifying the Six Steps, could I evaluate my response to adversity objectively, the way my mind worked while sitting in that waiting room. This evaluation taught me that I operated on fear. My knee-jerk response to adversity was a negative mindset. And from what I'd now learned, those who sank in adversity took the negative road. Those who soared took the positive. Remember, fear is only false evidence appearing real.

## Mindset Is Contagious

Still, negativity is the go-to response to trauma for most of us. Andy is a lawyer at our firm. All of his clients are dealing with some form of significant trauma. It is a draining line of work. We want to do everything we can to help people see the amazing opportunities ahead, to heal the people who come to us in so much anguish. We want to fix them, and of course we can't, so we feel useless. Even a big court win can't make up for the feeling of failure we experience when we go home at night. The feeling that we simply put a band-aid on our client's problem. We didn't heal it.

Last year I noticed Andy was changing. He seemed more unhappy and stressed. He was gaining weight, was no longer exercising. He was having difficulty sleeping, but he had to get sleep, so he started drinking alcohol to cure the insomnia. He would wake up sick, angry, and tired. I'd been there, during the time I was building the law firm, and I could see it clear as day. He was working with people living through the greatest pain of their lives, their own rock bottoms, and the pain was rubbing off on him. I wasn't unique.

Negative energy is contagious, not only because we strive to identify with those we care about, but also because we feel powerless to turn things around for those going through adversity. Andy was on the verge of giving up. Numbing the pain was easier than living in it. He started neglecting his own needs. He spiraled into a darker and darker worldview. *What's the point of even trying?* When people we care about are at their rock bottom, we begin to absorb their emotions. As social beings, the emotions of others infiltrate our thinking. We don't often recognize when it happens, and it's hard to escape. Have you ever felt your energy get sucked from other people's negative energy? Ask a person who performs bodywork on people. Energy is real.

Positive energy is equally contagious. It spreads like wildfire. And at this time in my life, years after my own struggles, I knew how to yank Andy off his current route and redirect him down the right one. Like I had once done, Andy was immersing himself in negative thoughts. He was sprinting down that path, unable to see anything but a dark and terrible world where horrible things happened to his clients. He absorbed the negativity. I took him aside, expressed my concern, and told him about an alternative, one he hadn't considered. I gave Andy the whole spiel, the Six Steps, emphasizing Step 3–Get Your Mind Right. Andy's situation was anything but helpless. His concern about his clients' wellbeing was not a threat to his life, but a challenge. If he could accept the challenge and apply the Six Steps, he could teach them to his clients and go home at night with a smile on his face. In turn, his clients could go home, put the Six Steps into practice, and teach them by example to their friends, parents, and children.

The six traits of those who thrive in adversity are easy to apply and rapidly effective, particularly Step 3. I instructed Andy to accept his rock bottom, embrace his desperation, work his way back to that fork in the road, and this time choose the positive path, the one with the flashlight, where opportunity becomes visible. He now had the opportunity to change the lives of his clients. Winning court cases was a side gig–the icing on the cake. The real reward of the job was changing his clients' way of life, and now he had the tools to accomplish just that. We are trauma lawyers. We don't have to adopt the trauma.

I saw his mindset changing before my eyes. Day one, Andy came to work with a newfound motivation. He'd accepted the challenge to change the situation. He was excited about it. I mean, what other options do we have? Saying this guy was transformed is an understatement. He became a top litigator and leader within our firm.

As with the negative path, when we're around someone who is walking the positive road, it can be nearly impossible not to join them. My wife, Katy, is like this. Like me, she is a seeker, but she seeks knowledge whereas I seek answers. There is a difference. I love Katy's mindset. She is very aware of her feelings, patient with others, comforting, and encouraging. When any of us stray, maybe blurt out something unkind, she reminds us to think first, to determine whether our words are necessary, kind, and truthful. She is my "Ambassador of Quan" (*Jerry Maguire* reference), a positive mindset guide and lemonade maker. And it rubs off on everyone around her.

I like to think that my overwhelming stress during those early years of the law firm and my frightening medical experience led me to change my mindset and my family's future. But it was those around me. Katy's positive mindset put me in the position to seek answers, to question why some individuals submit to adversity while others flourish. Katy's habit of continual improvement–no matter the circumstances–became a habit of my own.

I am very fortunate to be married to a happy person. Not all of us have this advantage. However, all of us can offer this advantage to our own friends and family. Adhering to the path of opportunity and solutions, even in difficult times, is irresistible to those around us. A true gift. The way we navigate life's journey impacts how we interact with our surroundings and how we experience this wild ride. Developing a positive mindset is a vital step in moving up and out of our rock bottoms. A positive mindset ensures that personal growth never stops, even when facing the most mammoth of obstacles.

## Remarkable Rebounds: Tiffany Haddish

[writing about an old photo of herself]: *"I look at this picture and want to cry tears of joy for this girl. I remember that night. She was homeless, hungry, scared, and hurt. I promised her if she kept faith in God and herself, we would get to a place where we will be housed, overfed, less hurt, and fear free."*[25]

Comedian Tiffany Haddish was raised by an abusive mother. She learned that being funny would distract her mother from hitting her. She was eventually placed in foster care and then raised by her grandmother. Later, homeless and living in her car, Haddish began seeking work as a stand-up comedian. She arrived late to events so people wouldn't know she lived in her car. One night Kevin Hart realized what she was doing. He gave her $300 for a motel room. She used that time in the comfort of the motel to write a list of goals. Nearly all of them have come true. Her stand-up career took off and she has starred in films like *Girls Trip and Night School*. She now has a net worth of $6 million.

25 Taylor DB. Tiffany Haddish recalls being 'homeless and scared' in Instagram post: 'I'm so happy we have come this far.' April 26, 2019. *New York Post*.

CHAPTER 8

# POSITIVITY VERSUS A RIGHT MIND

For most of us, once severe adversity enters the picture, default mode is a negative mindset. Default mode can last seconds, minutes, hours, months, years. At some point, we recognize we are in trouble, we're going down the wrong path. Learning to make this recognition early on, if not immediately, is key to coming out of trauma or adversity on top. The more we practice seeking opportunity and solutions when small challenges arise, the faster we are going to respond with the same mindset when the big one hits.

We pick up on and mimic the emotions of the people around us. For example, studies show that when we spend time with happy people, we tend to become happier.[26] When sports teams adopt a positive mindset as a group, the individual players tend to practice positivity themselves. Each positive friend you add to your network increases your chances of becoming happier by nine percent. The data is powerful. After reading numerous sports studies showing the same result, we immediately hired a mindset coach for the firm's lawyers and clients.

Likewise, if your coworkers or partners in life are depressed, you are more likely to be depressed. If fact, one study found that divorce is contagious.[27] People with a friend who gets divorced are 75 percent more likely to get

---

26 Fowler JH, Christakis NA. Dynamic spread of happiness in a large social network: longitudinal analysis over 20 years in the Framingham Heart Study. *BMJ* 2008;337:a2338.

27 McDermott R, Fowler JH, Christakis NA. Breaking Up is Hard to Do, Unless Everyone Else is Doing it Too: Social Network Effects on Divorce in a Longitudinal Sample. *Soc. Forces.* 2013 Dec; 92(2): 491–519.

divorced themselves. A shocking statistic and a wakeup call. If you want to save your marriage, surround yourself with people who are making it work despite imperfections. Scan for red flags among the emotional influencers in your life. Spend time with productive, opportunistic, resilient people.

Better yet. Marry up. Marriage isn't easy. It's less easy for someone like myself, whose father wasn't around and didn't prioritize them. That, alone, is traumatic. I'm a product of a divorce and, even today, I still see the damage it does to my soul. Katy, too, is a product of a divorce. We don't have a roadmap for marriage. Being married to someone who is constantly thinking about areas for improvement comes with a whole litany of problems. We grow as individuals. We have friends we grow close to or other relationships we allow to fade. As we age, we value time differently. We are less tolerant of wasting it. People grow apart.

There are certain qualities in people that contribute to lasting relationships. Take my wife Katy. I have been luckier than I deserve to have reconnected with my college sweetheart and married her in my late thirties. We are going on 13 years together. We are not the same people that got married in 2009. My wife and I built the beginnings of Burnham Law together. We worked hard to build a marriage, a home, and a business. When I think of all my failures, my complaining, my struggles with being a new stepfather, husband, father, boss, and legal entrepreneur, I am in awe of how strong, patient, tolerant, and supportive my partner remained. She always challenges me to think differently. She has stood by me as the firm has several times teetered on the brink, as I learned to go all-in, attacked my weaknesses, and continued to work on becoming a better version of me. She has always been there, patiently waiting for me to catch up. These are the qualities you want when choosing who to surround yourself with.

Easier said than done, right? All of us have friends and family who are negative. We're not about to abandon the people we love because they're going through a rough patch. Be there for them, listen, provide what you can. But when the negative energy starts flowing, do *not* participate. You have two choices. You can either dismiss yourself or turn the conversation around–whichever is easiest. Just put an end to it. Remember, negativity is highly contagious. No mask is going to help you here. Either remain six feet apart or destroy the negative energy then and there.

How do you turn the conversation around? Say you're sitting there chatting over lunch and your friend says, "I cannot control my son. I'm at my wits' end. He plays video games 24/7 and won't even speak to me." Normal lunchtime conversation, right? We hear it every day. Complaining breaks the ice. It's something to talk about. Do not participate. Either clear your dishes and get back to work or turn it around. Whatever you do, don't say, "Yeah, teenagers are hard."

If you want to turn it around, try, "Sounds like you have a genius on your hands," or, "all the creative, intelligent kids love video games. Great problem-solving skills." Your lunch partner may be shocked. Good. If they want to continue discussing their genius child, great. If they keep complaining, redirect or get out. Even the slightest negative energy surrounding us greatly impacts the way we respond to adversity in our own lives. It isn't pretty. Let the positive people in your life have a greater influence over you. Transfer that positive energy to your loved ones, and everyone reaps the rewards.

My mother kicked my father out of the house when I was an infant. Her father (my grandfather, who I never met) abandoned the family when she was a teenager. She coped with stress by smoking cigarettes for decades, working for the New York State Division for Youth as a social worker dealing with traumatic, deplorable, and sad family situations. She developed COPD and struggled to breathe for years. And yet she managed to invest in the lives of those around her and was always positive. One of many reasons why she was my hero. She was making lemonade for years without me realizing it.

## Beware False Message Blindness

Step 3 isn't about posting smiling photos on social media, laughing with our children in a pumpkin patch on Thanksgiving with our new fall outfits. That ain't it. Social media can be toxic in that way. It represents a false reality. Not many are willing to post a photo arguing with their spouses or sitting in a pile of Kleenex sobbing over a job termination. But we all experience times of hardship and trauma. Getting our mind right during adversity does not mean disguising ourselves. It's not about smiling, acting, or repeating positive affirmations, habits that can quickly become forms of denial and distraction. Getting your mind right means embracing the challenge at hand and getting excited about seeking solutions.

Those I've known who've been diagnosed with cancer offer a nice example of the fine line that exists between "positive thinking" and "getting your mind right." Any cancer patient knows the go-to motivational message from social media, friends, and family: "We're going to beat this. You're a warrior. Cancer doesn't stand a chance against you!" (note that no doctor will ever utter these words). While messages like these certainly feel empowering, they don't cure cancer. If they did, millions of oncologists would be out of a job. Studies show that a positive mindset has no physical impact on the outcome of cancer.[28]

The reality is, none of us know when our time is up. A person with stage-four cancer who's been given three months to live could die in a car wreck tomorrow on the way to chemo. None of us are guaranteed three

28 Andrade G. The ethics of positive thinking in healthcare. *J Med Ethics Hist Med.* 2019; 12:18.

months, or even three hours. We must take what we are facing right at this moment and *use* it to create change. During your months of chemotherapy and radiation therapy, rather than focusing on how great life will be once you beat cancer, focus on how you can take your diagnosis and turn it into something golden right now. Embrace the experience. Cancer teaches us all how very valuable every moment in life is. For those who beat it, money, fame, and prestige pale in comparison to the beauty of being able to walk outside in the sunshine with a loved one. A cancer diagnosis is an opportunity, not a threat. The challenge is not to "beat cancer," but to *use* it to your benefit–whether that be teaching those around you to cherish every moment, mapping out how you plan to move forward *with or without* cancer, or documenting your experience in a manuscript to share what you are learning with the world.

We can't change our circumstances, but we *can* change the effect our circumstances have on our lives. Like Pat Riley says: "*Shoulda, coulda, and woulda won't get it done. In attacking adversity, only a positive attitude, alertness, and regrouping to basics can launch a comeback.*"[29] Getting our mind right means recognizing what we are facing and getting busy using that obstacle in a productive way. Not denying it or pretending it will all work out, or distracting ourselves from reality. Use the obstacle itself. Don't waste precious time blinded by distraction.

## But What About Hope?

Research has shown that hope is a predictive factor when it comes to positivity, success, and longevity.[30] Additionally, people who have hope

29 Riley, Pat. (1993). *Winner Within Success*. Putnam Publishing Group.

30 Long KNG, Kim ES, Chen Y, et al. The role of Hope in subsequent health and well-being for older adults: An outcome-wide longitudinal approach. *Global Epidemiology*. Vol. 2, 2020. 100018.

experience less depression and anxiety. Hope is a powerful feeling. It gives us the extra kick to press onward in the face of adversity.

Hope has been a powerful force in my rebound from traumas. When I sat in my basement learning everything there was to know about Colorado family law so I wouldn't blow my career up, I did it because I had the hope that I could. I could learn. I could be a success. I leaned on my experience in lacrosse. I started lacrosse in high school, later than most kids in the lacrosse hotbed of Syracuse, New York. It wasn't easy. But anytime I felt swamped, slammed by monster wave after monster wave, my competitive nature pushed me forward. I refused to drown. Hope binds with desperation. Desperation says "This is as bad as it gets. We might as well try everything." Hope then chimes in with, "It's going to get better. One of these things we try will work." Hope keeps you moving forward, believing that something will change. Hope drives the grind.

It is important to distinguish between hope and its close cousin, optimism. Hope is more goal-oriented, while optimism is more open to any number of possibilities. Take a hopeful person waiting to hear whether they got an important job promotion. Hope is the calm and comforting friend that will accompany them during the wait. But what happens to hope when they hear that Frank got the promotion, not them? It is gone, only to return when they set a new goal to look forward to.

An optimist would like the promotion, sure, but optimism doesn't disappear when we don't reach a goal. An optimist knows that when one door closes, another one (often a better one) opens. Optimism doesn't rely on reaching a goal as much as it relies on a solution eventually presenting itself. When a person is in the right mind frame, they will be both optimistic and hopeful in the face of adversity. Optimism and hope are some nice side effects of getting your mind right. Once you choose the positive path, seeking opportunities and solutions, hope and optimism creep in and walk alongside you, traits that make the journey doable, even enjoyable.

Hope isn't only a side effect of getting our mind right. It can also act as a guide, helping to lead us off the negative road and onto the positive one. If you can muster up some hope, a positive mindset will begin to snowball. But how does a hopeless individual find hope? For one, we can look back at past accomplishments. Was there a tough time in your past when you were able to push through and come out relatively unscathed? Why should this tough time be any different? You can also create your own small victories. What seems impossible to you right this minute? Getting out of bed? Toss your covers off, stand up, pace the room a bit. There you go. That is success right there, even if you crawl right back in bed, you literally succeeded in your goal. And if you can do that, you can do anything. You have hope. Even the smallest of victories spur hope. We are just looking for a bit of momentum here.

Another powerful way to gather up some hope is to shift your expectations and goals. Switch it up. Be the optimist. Understand that there are a multitude of possibilities out there, thousands with positive outcomes–not just the one possibility you are hoping for. If you've just filed for bankruptcy, holding out hope that you'll make a million dollars next year might do more harm than good. But shooting to pay your living expenses next month could totally happen. And if even that looks rough, what's wrong with purchasing a camper and living the adventurous life of travel? Now we can see a little hope creeping in. You are never limited to a single option. Think outside the box.

## Physical Reactions to Stress

A report examining over 300 studies over 30 years concluded that stress impacts our immune system in either a negative or positive way, depending on whether the stress is chronic or acute.[31] Brief periods of stress associated with things like public speaking or making an urgent decision while driving in traffic triggers the fight or flight response and boosts the immune system. Our body detects a sudden stress and releases the chemicals necessary to overcome the stress, amping up our ability to fight off infection (anticipating injury), speeding our thought processes, strengthening our decision-making capacity, and fueling our muscles to perform superhuman feats.

On the other hand, chronic stress can damage our health. Stretching the extreme chemical response to stress over long periods of time can deteriorate our immune system, slow our thought processes, weaken our decision-making capacity, and harm our body tissue. As mentioned earlier, I went through it. Andy went through it. People who live in a domestic violence situation go through it. People who lose multiple loved ones in a short span of time. All are chronic stress situations. The body simply cannot keep up.

When we're existing under chronic stress, our body begins to preserve resources, shutting down every system it can while still sustaining life. Our immune system is one of the first to go, subjecting us to illnesses and diseases that would be a non-issue in a healthy state. Chronic stress puts the body in a dangerous situation.

The chronic stress of moving to a new state with a new family, a new career, and little money in the midst of a recession took me down. I wasn't going to quit mentally, so my body forced me to quit. Next thing I know

31 Segerstrom SC, Miller GE. Psychological Stress and the Human Immune System: A Meta-Analytic Study of 30 Years of Inquiry. *Psychol Bull.* 2004 Jul; 130(4): 601–630.

I can't even walk and am diagnosed with Guillain-Barré. I think about chronic stress and the years that I floundered around trying to build a firm. I fought the whole way, let small failures destroy my psyche, and grinded until my body quit. Had I got my mind right, taken the positive path, seen the many opportunities available to me, the ride would have been much, much smoother. But I didn't know then what I know now.

Today, I practice the six traits of those I've seen thrive in adversity. I changed my approach, which fed into positive growth, better leadership, attracting talent, developing talent, growing practice areas, opening eight offices in two states, embracing failures as opportunities, becoming a leader focusing on firm leaders and their successes, investing in people, and sharing my experiences as a form of service. We could say my MS scare was the best thing that happened to the firm and me as a human being. Today, I am retired from the firm at the age of 50. I'm a stay-at-home dad. I live a completely different life, and it consists primarily of engaging and investing my time in my family.

When I decided to leave the management of the firm in November 2020, my plan was to live on Kauai for four months, go with the flow and see what happens. I wanted to see what trusting our Managing Partner, Stephanie, felt like. I changed my intent, which changed my life. And it continues to change. I keep seeking growth, I keep failing and succeeding. I'm an ongoing work in progress and embracing every minute. For now, my health is great. And if someday it isn't, I'm certain I will be able to use that new experience to grow. I can't help but blame the elimination of chronic stress on getting my mind right.

There are plenty of studies showing that chronic stress is a leading contributor to cancer.[32] For example, studies show that people who suffer

---

32 Dai S, Mo Y, Wang Y, et al. Chronic Stress Promotes Cancer Development. *Front Oncol.* 2020 Aug 19;10:1492.

from negative thoughts throughout stressful situations have a reduction in killer cells,[33] the cells in our bodies that hunt and kill cancerous cells. On the flip side, individuals who carried optimistic outlooks throughout stressful situations did not show a reduction in killer cells. The stress itself contributes to disease, but the way we think during stress can either amplify or reduce our risk for disease. We may not be able to control the stressors in our life, but we can control the way we think about them.

## Charitable Acts Improve Mental State

Positivity just feels good. Think about how you feel after you do something selfless, like working in a soup kitchen, feeding your neighbor's cat, donating $5 to your friend's Facebook birthday fundraiser, or making your girlfriend's favorite meal. Doing good makes you feel good and breeds positive thoughts. You get what you give. When you are working on building your positive mindset, keep this in mind. If you feel stuck in yourself and your crap, break out by doing something positive for someone else.

Studies show that altruism (doing selfless acts for others) lowers blood pressure, increases longevity, reduces depression, lowers stress, and increases self-esteem.[34] Doing things for other people does good things for you, both mentally and physically.

On April 27, 2021, my mother died. She was my hero, my safety net, my one constant. Every time a bad thing ever happened in my life, I remember my mother being there. My mother cared so much about others, their lives and dreams. She never wavered in her warrior spirit despite suffering from COPD for decades. It has not been easy. I've had my ups and downs. As

33 Dragoş D, Tănăsescu MD. The effect of stress on the defense systems. *J Med Life.* 2010 Feb 15; 3(1): 10–18.

34 Yeung JWK, Zhang Z, Kim TY. Volunteering and health benefits in general adults: cumulative effects and forms. *BMC Public Health.* 2018; 18: 8.

time went by, I felt closer to her. I felt a sense of purpose. I started a pro bono division of Burnham Law in her name, the Nancy Burnham Equal Justice Project, created in her memory to provide funding for those below the poverty line to receive quality legal representation. To help fund this charity, I created ToddBurnham.com, a website that provides guidance and support for lawyers and entrepreneurs in the service industry. It is what I know–how to build and grow a law firm (or any service business). And being of service to others in my field, even competitors, has improved my mental state dramatically. Try it. It works. I've found the best way to defeat grief is to replace it with gratitude. I feel more grateful when I am helping others.

## Make Positivity a Habit

Creating a positive mental mindset must become a habit. *Webster's Dictionary* defines a habit as "something that a person does often in a regular and repeated way." Adopting a positive mindset requires you to have positive thoughts regularly. To be most effective, you want them to be automatic, something your mind learns to do without having to try. You want to condition your mind to think positively.

You've probably heard of Pavlov's study with dogs.[35] Pavlov gave the dogs food which resulted in salivating. Then when he gave the dogs food, he added in the sound of a bell. Soon the dogs came to associate the sound of the bell with the food and when they heard it, they would salivate, even if there wasn't any food present. Pavlov trained the dogs' bodies and brains to associate the bell with food. Salivating for the bell became an ingrained

35 Pavlov, PI. *Conditioned reflexes: An investigation of the physiological activity of the cerebral cortex.* (Translated by G. V. Anrep) (1927). London: Allen and Unwin.

response. The dogs certainly didn't think about it. Their bodies just responded.

This is what we want to do with positive thinking. It needs to simply become our automatic response to things we experience, even adversity and trauma. But how do we create a habit and make it stick? If you've ever tried a weight loss or fitness program, you know it can be hard to create new habits. Here are several tips to help ease the process.

- **Start with simple habits.** Pick small things that are not challenging so you can get used to building new habits. For example, stepping outside each morning, looking at the sky, and thinking how lucky you are to be alive is a small and easy act to incorporate in your daily routine. Before you know it, you'll be pattering outside in your slippers each morning without even thinking.

- **Start with short time spans.** If you feel meditation is a habit you'd like to try, don't schedule 15 minutes on your first day. Don't set up a special spot or room in your house. Ease into it. Sit up in bed, set a timer for two minutes, take ten deep breaths. Each day, add a minute, add some techniques, add some new locations. If you miss a day, go back to the easier location or shorter time span. Trick your mind into accepting the new habit by making it easy and brief.

- **Physical actions are easier to make into habits than mental actions**. There's no fooling yourself with actual physical acts. Either you do them or you don't. There's also no internal discussion about it. If you made it a habit to draw the drapes each night, you either do it or you don't. And you can't say to yourself, "well, I drew the drapes halfway, it's close enough" because it is objectively not the same. Physical habits are powerful because they are linked to actual motion. So, to incorporate mental changes, link them with physical habits. When you fill your coffee cup each morning, make it a habit to list what you want to accomplish that day. When you brush your teeth, make it a habit to review the progress you have made. Always examine how far you've come, not how far you have yet to go. If you start thinking about how far you have to go, stop thinking and start doing.

- **Habits are easier when you have a partner**. Many people have "goal buddies" for things like weight loss or working out. This year I started a "Winter Challenge," a firm-wide competition for those wanting to get active, a supportive network. Emails going back and forth at 6:00 a.m., people talking smack, inspiring each other, is now commonplace at the firm. On some level, it's peer pressure. But it's also about having other people to relate to, who identify with the struggle and the rewards. Going to AA helps drinkers to stay on the wagon because they have the support of other people who are on the same journey. Finding supportive and positive people to work with during adversity can help you stick with the habits you are trying to build.

- **Adding visual and auditory cues make habits easier to maintain.** Similar to physical motion, visual and auditory cues can trigger you to think certain thoughts. If you want to build a habit of praising yourself for some small accomplishment each day, do it every time you hear the water running for your shower. Associate that sound with praise. Soon, you'll be patting yourself on the back throughout the day by accident.

- **If you want to change a habit you already have, replace it with another habit.** If you're already in the habit of doing one thing, substitute it with another habit rather than building a whole new habit into your daily routine. Instead of obsessing every day over the low numbers in your bank account, take the time that you usually use to look at your bank account online and use that time to instead Google one step you can take today that will help you improve your finances. You're simply swapping one thing out for another. it will fit into your day in the same place, relying on the same cues that prompt you to do the unhealthy habit.

## Positive Mental Habits to Adopt

There are five specific habits that, once incorporated into our lives, can help boost our resilience and ability to maintain a positive direction during adversity.

### 1. Mindfulness

Mindfulness is a five-dollar word for living in the present. To be mindful, we focus on what is in front of us right now, at this moment in time. We tune into what we can see, feel, hear, taste, touch, smell, and experience right now where we are at this moment. We are not existing in the past. That is over and gone. We are not existing in the future either. That will come on its own. So, we don't allow our mind to think about anything from the past or the future. The only thing we can really experience and influence at the moment is the present. All of our thoughts, senses, and awareness are focused only on the moment we are living in right now.

Mindfulness can be incredibly freeing—we don't realize how hard our mind is working at evaluating all the things that have happened and all the possible paths ahead of us until we turn that volume down and hear ONLY the now. A key part of mindfulness is simply letting ourselves be in this moment without judging, criticizing, or analyzing anything. So, think about what you are doing, seeing, and feeling now, without judging any part of it. It's OK to recognize feelings and thoughts as they pop up, but then just let them go without engaging with them. I watch Katy living this way. I, of course, remain a work in progress.

Studies show that practicing mindfulness reduces pain and illness.[36] Other studies suggest that mindfulness improves personal relationships.[37] Mindfulness simplifies your life and makes you better able to cope in all areas. Focusing on the now means you are only dealing with your physical symptoms at this second (not what you have suffered in the past or what you might be dealing with in the years to come). There's just less to worry about. The same is true for relationships. When you are focused only on today, you're not reliving conflict from yesterday or worrying about where it's all going in the future.

Living in the present allows you to let go of your stress about what could happen tomorrow or what you might have done wrong yesterday. It simplifies things because all you have to do is what is in front of you right now. You're not responsible for anything else. Stress evaporates

---

36 Zeidan F, Vago DR. Mindfulness meditation-based pain relief: a mechanistic account. *Ann N Y Acad Sci.* 2016;1373(1):114-127.

37 Kappen G, Karremans JC, Burk WJ, Buyukcan-Tetik A. *On the Association Between Mindfulness and Romantic Relationship Satisfaction: the Role of Partner Acceptance.* Mindfulness (NY). 2018;9(5):1543-1556.

when you are able to be in a mindful state. Because of this, mindfulness by its very nature is a positive mental mindset.

**2. Management of Negative Thoughts**

No matter how positive your mindset, you will still be faced with negative thoughts from time to time. That's normal, particularly as you are climbing up out of your rock bottom. Negative thoughts are going to appear. Here are some ways to deal with those negative thoughts.

- **Identify them.** You can't get rid of them if you can't see them. Pick apart what you are thinking and identify the thoughts that are negative. Don't let them linger in your subconscious. Call them out front and center and label them as negative.

- **Challenge them.** Instead of seeing your negative thoughts as fact, label them as opinions, bad, unfounded opinions. You wouldn't agree with a stranger telling you negative things about yourself. So, challenge your own negativity. Realize that negative thoughts are not facts, then counteract them with an equal and opposite positive spin.

- **Give the thought a time limit.** Set a timer and allow yourself to engage with that negative thought for three minutes. When the time is up, move on to other thoughts. You give it its due, but refuse to let it overstay its welcome.

- **Stop judging yourself.** We are often harsher when we judge ourselves than in how we think about other people. Silence the inner critic. Tell them to take a seat. You don't need to hear their negative opinions. In fact, those opinions are ridiculous.

- **Think about your strengths.** Focusing on what you are good at, what you can do, and where your skills lie will help provide a barrier against negativity.

### 3. Meditation

Meditation is a practice that is linked to mindfulness, but it requires a specific practice every single day. It is a calming and stilling of the mind that creates a unique mental state (it's called the parasympathetic mental state) with a variety of benefits. If you don't know how to meditate, check out Mindful.org or the Headspace series on Netflix for tips. You can also check out the book *Ten Percent Happier* by Dan Harris, which is about how one journalist started meditating and found improved happiness because of it. There are also tons of YouTube videos about meditation to help you get started. Meditation should become one of your positive habits.

Meditation has many benefits:[38] improved memory and learning, reduction in negative thoughts, improved mental capacity, reduced negative emotions, healthier relationships, reduced anxiety, improved creativity, improved clarity,[39] and improved sleep.[40] Every single thing on that list is something you need when you are trying to come back from the trauma of being at rock bottom.

---

38 Ngô TL. Review of the effects of mindfulness meditation on mental and physical health and its mechanisms of action. *Sante Ment Que.* 2013 Autumn;38(2):19-34.

39 Pragya SU, Mehta ND, Abomoelak B, et al. Effects of Combining Meditation Techniques on Short-Term Memory, Attention, and Affect in Healthy College Students. *Front Psychol.* 2021 Mar 5;12:607573.

40 Rusch HL, Rosario M, Levison LM, et al. The effect of mindfulness meditation on sleep quality: a systematic review and meta-analysis of randomized controlled trials. *Ann NY Acad Sci.* 2019 Jun;1445(1):5-16.

Physically, research has shown that meditation can: enhance immune function; lessen the symptoms of chronic fatigue syndrome, irritable bowel syndrome, and menopause; reduce inflammation; produce higher levels of serotonin and melatonin; boost quality of life for chronic pain and fibromyalgia patients; lessen cravings in substance abuse disorder; and ease adaptation to cancer diagnoses.[41]

Studies suggest that meditation affects the body and mind by altering various regions in the brain.[42] For example:

- Attention regulation through meditation may affect the anterior cingulate cortex (attention, emotional expression, mood regulation)

- Emotion regulation through meditation may affect modulation of the amygdala (fear response) by the lateral prefrontal cortex (cognitive control, memory, attentional selection, planning, reward response)

- Body awareness through meditation may affect the insula (pain perception, heart rate, respiratory rate) and temporoparietal junction (empathy, compassion)

- Cognitive re-evaluation through meditation may activate the dorsal medial prefrontal cortex (error processing, cognitive control, conflict monitoring)

---

41 Ngô TL. Review of the effects of mindfulness meditation on mental and physical health and its mechanisms of action. *Sante Ment Que.* 2013 Autumn;38(2):19-34.

42 Ngô TL. Review of the effects of mindfulness meditation on mental and physical health and its mechanisms of action. *Sante Ment Que.* 2013 Autumn;38(2):19-34.

- Flexible self-concept in meditation may affect the prefrontal median cortex (attention, inhibitory control, habit formation, long-term memory), posterior cingulated cortex (computes the context from which stimuli emerge), insula (pain, heart rate, respiratory rate), and temporoparietal junction (empathy, compassion)

- Exposure, extinction, and reconsolidation in meditation may affect the ventromedial prefrontal cortex (emotional processing, memory, decision-making, social cognition, self-perception), hippocampus (learning, memory), and amygdala (fear response).

If you've never tried it, meditation might seem a bit crunchy or weird. But people have been practicing mediation since the beginning of time. Have you ever sat in front of a campfire, staring into the flames, and just existed? That is a natural, innate form of meditation. It's a proven ancient practice that anyone can do easily. Meditation is a turning inward of your mind and a slowing of your breathing. Mindfulness is incorporated in the practice. It doesn't cost anything and takes very little time. You can do it anywhere (although it's best to start out somewhere quiet where you won't be interrupted). And you can't do it wrong. Just go for it. Even five minutes a day total is enough to create significant change in thought patterns and performance. Watch a quick lesson online, set the timer on your phone, and give it a shot.

**4. Spirituality**

Spirituality is not necessarily religion (though it can be). When I speak of spirituality, I'm talking about connecting to a higher power or broader meaning. You don't have to join a specific religion or pray or even believe in a god to engage in spirituality. You simply must consider some kind of meaning and purpose in the universe. Seek out feelings of peace, love, awe, gratitude, connection, forgiveness, and inspiration.

Many studies have been conducted on the benefits of spirituality[43] and concluded that those who practice some form of spirituality show increases in longevity, general happiness, life satisfaction, physical health, and reduction in stress. If you're at a tough place in your life, this could be the thing that helps you move forward.

Becoming spiritual might sound like a massive life change, but it's something you can do fairly easily with just a few simple adjustments to your life:

- **Start small.** Choose tiny steps you can take that increase your connection to the world, to a god, to other people, or to the universe. Something as small as taking one minute a day to breathe and look at the night sky can do it. I'm serious.

- **Decide.** Decide that this is something you are committed to and that it is an important part of your life. Once you start to identify yourself as spiritual or religious, you've already changed an important label and will take actions that fit it.

- **Commit time**. Commit to something you can do every day that will increase your spiritual practice. This could include reading something about spiritualty, journaling your thoughts, talking to

43 Dragan, D., McDuffie, D., Crowther, M.R. (2020). Health Benefits of Spirituality. In: Uribarri, J., Vassalotti, J. (eds) Nutrition, Fitness, and Mindfulness. Nutrition and Health. Humana, Cham.

others, praying, meditating, or practicing gratitude, good deeds, or forgiveness.

- **Explore.** Be open to learning and growing in spirituality. Take steps to get more knowledge or different perspectives about it. Sample a lot of options and test out different approaches to find what works for you.

- **Connect.** It can be helpful to connect with others who are on the same journey, whether this is clergy, gurus, friends, or simply people who write books or make videos about it. Having a community of people who share your beliefs and can support you will make the journey easier.

**5. Gratitude**

Gratitude is about feeling thankful for whatever you have and whatever is going a little bit right in your life (you can find something, I promise you). A gratitude practice can be as simple as taking a few moments to think about what you have to be grateful for, or it could become a daily or weekly practice of journaling and making lists of things to be grateful for. Some people post once a day on social media with the small thing they are grateful for that day.

Gratitude does not have to mean thanking or recognizing other people for their impact on your life, but it can include that. Some people write thank you notes as part of their gratitude practice. Other people make an effort to take a moment and thank people (even people like cashiers or health care aides that they have passing contact with) for what they do. Gratitude can be encompassed in your spirituality practice, if you make the time to thank a god, higher power, or the universe for what you have–food, health, clothing, a roof over your head.

Gratitude has incredible positive impacts on happiness. Studies show that gratitude practices change our brains.[44] It might seem like people who have a lot to be grateful for would benefit the most from this. Having a lot of great things happening in your life would make it easy to feel gratitude and to experience benefits. However, even people who are experiencing tough times, struggling with depression, who at first glance may not seem to have a lot to be grateful for, reap numerous benefits from gratitude practices. In fact, gratitude helps some people more than conventional therapy.

People who practice gratitude show changes in the part of their brain associated with learning and decision-making. Not only do gratitude practices make us feel better and happier, but they improve our decision-making and ability to learn new concepts, important survival tools when you are pulling yourself out of trauma and creating a path forward.

Gratitude is a small, easy way to make massive positive change in your life. Remember to focus only on what you have to be grateful for, not what you are stressed or worried about. As with everything in this book, start small. Be grateful for your pillow. Believe me, there are billions of people in the world who don't have one. Be grateful for your sight, your ability to hear. Be grateful for the sunshine, books, dogs, medicine, fruit, your favorite movie. You'll be surprised at how long your list becomes.

---

44 Wong YJ, Owen J, Gabana NT, et al. Does gratitude writing improve the mental health of psychotherapy clients? Evidence from a randomized controlled trial, *Psychotherapy Research.* 2018. 28:2, 192-202.

## Get Help When You Need It

These tools and practices can be helpful, but many of us also need the aid of professional mental health counselors or medical care. Seeking out a counselor or doctor can be your golden ticket to a successful and productive future. If you are suffering from a mental health disorder, you can't positive-think your way out of it, just like you can't cure cancer or diabetes with positive thoughts. Depression, anxiety, PTSD, eating disorders, bipolar disorder, require professional assistance. Level that playing field! Once you've got that squared away, you will be equipped to move onward and upward. Just like a diabetic uses insulin and an amputee uses a prosthetic, if you're suffering from mental illness or suspect you might be, a therapist can provide the assistance you need. *See Appendix: Mental Health Resources.* From there, the sky is the limit.

The same holds true for any physical ailment or addiction. You must first deal with the illness itself through rehabilitation, medical care, a 12-Step program, and any required treatment before you can begin to build back from a rock bottom. Take care of your health first. It takes a sound mind to make your comeback. The Six Steps are your pathway forward *after* you prepare your physical and spiritual self for the fight.

## Build Intent

Carlos Ghosn, CEO of Nissan, took over the company in 1999. It was doing poorly at the time. No one believed in the brand. He clearly said he was going to turn the company around in one year. He stated his intent. Within a year, the business was profitable. Nissan is now one of the most profitable companies in the world.

Intent gives your positive mindset direction and a purpose. A positive mindset alone can improve your health, lessen stress, and help you avoid a massive array of unnecessary obstacles. But to move forward, you must harness your positive mindset with intent. What do you want to accomplish? Set small goals at first, then get more daring. By creating intent, and stating that intent, writing it down, you begin to notice when opportunity crosses your path. Without intent, opportunity is still there, but it isn't nearly as visible. Know what you are working for. Set a goal for today. Another for a week from today. Keep it simple but create intent.

## Small Steps Are Productive Steps

We'll hit on this topic in more detail later in the book, but it is important to point out that we are often overly critical of where our positive mindset is at. If you're walking down the street and you find a dime, you may think, "Damn, it's my lucky day!" Cool. You're 10 cents richer. You might step onto the subway with a smile on your face and, in a great mood, ask the guy next to you about the book he's reading. Turns out the guy with the book is hiring people in your field. Don't think finding that dime didn't have anything to do with your new prospective job offer. That right there is a big opportunity you would never have been open to if you hadn't let finding that dime spark your positive mindset.

But our logical minds tend to criticize these little victories. If we don't get our mind right, we might find a dime on the street and say, "Well this isn't going to help much with my bankruptcy." It's a logical thought. It's also a debilitating mindset. Positive thoughts about even the smallest things matter. They lay the groundwork, building up your positive mindset into a force able to tackle the bigger things.

During the more challenging times in our lives, we may only be able to find small things to feel positive about–and that's OK! Do it! Practice your positive mindset every chance you get. Nothing is too small to spark opportunity, creativity, and solutions. Pick up the dime and enjoy.

Developing a positive mindset takes practice. Do not let yourself feel negative about the fact that it will take some time for you to fully ingrain a positive mindset into your way of life. The best way to develop a positive mindset is to simply decide you're going to have one. Hold that principle foremost in your mind throughout your day. Every time you're faced with something where you feel yourself start to tilt into negativity, remind yourself: I have a positive mindset now!

## Remarkable Rebounds: Bethany Hamilton

*"Gratitude is a theme in my life. Appreciation is how I was able to quickly shift my mindset after losing my arm. Instead of focusing on what I didn't like about my body, or my limitations, I choose to be grateful for the remarkable body that I have."*[45]

Bethany Hamilton began surfing at age eight and was a talented, promising surfer at age 13 when she was attacked by a tiger shark off of Tunnels Beach in Kauai and lost an arm along with 60 percent of her blood. This was her rock bottom. Fast medical care saved her life. Within just two months, Hamilton was back on a surfboard, winning her first national surfing title. Hamilton went on to win many surfing titles, won Best Comeback Athlete ESPY, wrote a book about her experience (which was also made into a film that our daughters watched incessantly after meeting her) and competed on *The Amazing Race* and several other reality shows. She now has three children and runs a foundation and a life coaching business.

45 Hamilton B. [@bethanyhamilton]. (Nov. 12, 2020). Twitter.

CHAPTER 9

# POSITIVITY BUILDS A BETTER FUTURE

Remember those 40 minutes I spent waiting for my MRI, when I was overcome with panic and despair? That was one of those rock bottom moments where everything seems dark and there appears to be no light ahead. This all happened around the time that I hit my career rock bottom–not that day the Judge reprimanded me in the courtroom. Years later I found myself still trying to build a new life for myself and my family, yet everything was falling apart professionally, and I was facing a health crisis to boot. I recall telling my wife that I was miserable and didn't want to be a lawyer anymore.

I was living through a really terrible block of time. I look back on that part of my life as a big black smudge on the calendar. Painful and depressing. But I got out of it. And when people ask me to pinpoint one specific tool that helped me pull myself up and move forward, I say, hands-down, meditation. After meditating for just a few weeks, it became a practice I cannot live without. It changed the way I react to every situation in my life–both personally and professionally. Sometimes it is an active meditation. Sometimes it is just focusing on my breath rather than losing composure.

## Case Study: Malik

While Malik was in jail, he decided it was time to get his mind right. I'd Tony Robbins-ed the Six Steps into his brain, and he decided to take those 30 days and recreate his approach to life. I convinced him to try meditation. He gave it a shot, learned how to do meditative breathing, but found that for him, prayer was the most effective tool. He honed his spirituality and prayed several times a day, reaping the same benefits as I did with meditation.

He heard what I told him about mindfulness and decided that during those 30 days he could only live in each moment. He could not fix the past. He could not proceed with his future yet. So, he worked at experiencing the moment he had been given. He embraced that approach. Each minute behind bars was just that, one minute.

Though he was worried about how his plans for his dad would work out, he wrangled those negative thoughts and focused on the positive. He practiced being grateful for the people who were pitching in and helping. He recognized their help as an amazing gift and appreciated it. He started thinking of five other things to be grateful for each day, then said a prayer of thanks for them. He told me that one of the things he was grateful for was his DUI. This adverse situation forced him to clean up his act, reevaluate his life, and look for a new path forward.

He took his 30 days as his chance to rework the wiring in his brain. He already knew that he wanted to go to culinary school, so he thought about that and visualized his success. He believed in himself and talked himself through his future. He created intent, while remaining grounded in the moment, becoming a stronger, healthier person, building a positive mindset.

## Be Coffee

I can't say I don't struggle with keeping a right mind frame. Again, I'm a work in progress. I can see I've hit bottom, I can embrace my desperation, but sometimes I just can't reel in that inner critic. The concept of "Be Coffee," our firm's core message, always gets me back on track. It comes from the old parable of the carrot, the egg, and the coffee bean.

As the story goes, a young woman visited her mother with a heavy heart. Life was rough, and she was tired of struggling. She didn't know if she could go on. Her mother led her to the kitchen where three pots were boiling on the stove. One pot of carrots, one pot of eggs, and one pot of coffee beans. "What do you see?" the mother asked. "Carrots, eggs, and coffee," the daughter replied. "Notice the softness of the carrots?" the mother said, poking them with a fork. "And the hardness of the eggs?" as she peeled off the shell. Then she poured some coffee into a mug for her daughter, who sipped it and smiled as she tasted the rich roast.

"So?" the daughter replied.

"So, the three items have all faced tremendous adversity–the boiling water," said the mother. "But each reacted to that boiling water very differently. The once strong and hearty carrot came out soft and weak. And the once delicate egg became hardened inside. But the coffee beans responded differently. They changed nothing about themselves. Instead, they changed the boiling water around them, transforming their adverse surroundings into the rich and flavorful coffee you are now enjoying."

Be coffee. When you are facing adversity, don't let it weaken you or harden your spirit. Instead, keep your strong and sensitive nature and transform the adversity itself into something wonderful. If you are having trouble maintaining your positive mindset, remember to "be coffee." Rather than working to change your own nature, focus on changing the circumstances that surround you. This concept perfectly embodies my mother's spirit, and I told the story at her funeral, urging us all to be like Nancy in our lives. Be coffee.

## Meditation Became My Go-To

Meditation is my magic bullet. It calms my mind and my body. It releases stress. It allows me to focus on a single moment in time. It gives me mental and emotional strength. It has improved my health, my personal life, my professional life, and my entire mental attitude. If you do nothing else suggested in this book, I ask that you try meditation. In my opinion, it is one thing that is guaranteed to change your life no matter who you are or what you are dealing with. It's a one-size-fits-all cure.

Once I'd found meditation and started to feel the effects in my daily life, I felt deeply compelled to help other people tackle their own struggles. I started evaluating friends, family, coworkers, past clients, current clients, who had been through major challenges in their life journey. Meditation drove me to ask questions and seek answers. Why were some people able to turn things around? What did they have in common? That's where the Six Steps came from. Meditation did all of this for me. And to be clear, I'm not my wife. I still struggle with meditation. My thoughts begin to swirl around like mischievous goldfish, and I'm always having to come back to focus on my breathing. But it is enjoyable and beneficial just trying to get it right.

Meditation worked so well for me that I suggested one of my law partners to give it a try when I noticed he was feeling down. He's a meditating fool now. His division of the firm grew 40 percent since he strengthened his mindset through meditation. He experienced such an impact on his life that he now helps his own employees learn to meditate. If I didn't believe in the power of meditation before this, his life-pivot sealed it for me.

Meditation helped both of us accept what we were dealt and transform it to focus on the lemonade, not the lemons. As lawyers, we often find ourselves in the midst of very unhappy situations. We are surrounded by people experiencing trauma. I have found that instead of wallowing in the trauma, the way forward is to always approach everything with a positive mindset. Part of that means being open to change. If a client is in a traumatic situation, I help them see opportunity that will move them forward. When I am feeling caught in negativity, I seek opportunity. Andy started doing that too. A simple change in mindset allowed us to become better lawyers, not only able to win cases, but able to make a positive impact on the lives of our clients. When strategic planning with others, I tell everyone who will listen, "We are throwing where the receiver will be, not where they are right now." Same goes with life. Our clients' current situation is not permanent. Nothing is permanent. Think about where you are at in life, get desperate, and get your mind right.

## The Snowball Effect

I'd been living in Colorado for five years and my stress level was off the charts. Everyone I worked with and spoke to was stressed. I thought, what am I doing? I felt like a dumpster fire myself, trying to help people extinguish their own dumpster's fire. And a lot of other lawyers I knew felt the same way. This was no way to practice law. This is no way to live. The field I'd entered into with passion and gusto had turned dark and dismal. Did it have to be that way? There was no way that this level of stress was 'just part of the job.' Something wasn't right.

Before I changed my life by getting my mind right, I often told clients what they *wanted* to hear about their case along with my honest evaluation.

I was afraid of losing them. I couldn't build a successful practice if I lost clients. For example, in my practice as a divorce attorney, I work with parents who are in the middle of difficult custody cases. The parents sling mud at each other. They accuse the other person of terrible things. In my early years, when a client came in ranting about their horrible soon-to-be-ex who cheated on them and is a bad father, I might say, "Great, buckle up! We'll restrict him and show the court what a terrible father he is." After all, making the client feel like they are in the right means they will continue working with me, right? I took the client where they were at emotionally, tethered in, and accompanied them on their pre-plotted course through battle. Every day. And if I wasn't supervising an associate, drafting a motion, or preparing for trial, I would be on the phone speaking to potential new clients. My day ended around 10 pm and started at 6 am.

Strangely, once I developed a meditation practice, I found myself telling clients what they *needed* to hear. In the realm of divorce law, mudslinging is fatal. The courts want to see a responsible, respectful adult. The hateful, vengeful ex isn't near as likely to get what they're asking for. In the eyes of the Judge, hateful, vengeful folks aren't behaving rationally. They aren't prioritizing their children. It doesn't matter who is the better parent in real life. In the courtroom, the parent who causes drama is going to be examined with a fine-tooth comb. Every little flaw is magnified for the mentally unprepared spouse.

After a few weeks of meditation, I started giving people the advice that I would give a family member. I found myself explaining that a child and family investigation plus trial is going to take months, maybe years. The child is going to be the number one victim of any and all hatred directed toward the other parent. They will learn that the way to solve problems is by hurting other people, gossiping about them behind their backs, taking sides. Suddenly, when an angry husband entered my office ranting about his worthless wife, I was stopping him in his tracks and laying it out. Whatever he thought of his wife, he needed to turn it around, immediately. “Listen, if you want to get what you’re asking for, you cannot speak ill of your soon-to-be-ex–*at all.* Not to me, not to your partner, not to your children.” Almost immediately the firm started to organically grow. I became a legal strategist. I saw cases from the 30,000-foot view. I saw the whole field of the case. Soon I would begin applying the same lessons to the law practice.

Meditation had weakened my fear of losing clients, replacing it with confidence and security. When I spoke the truth to my clients, even when they didn’t want to hear it, I had a direct, clean impact on their lives. I guided them through a winning process, not necessarily a comfortable one. I gave it to them straight.

At first, I expected prospective clients to get up and walk out. Instead, many wanted to learn more. While some people cannot let themselves hear that truth, most are appreciative. And if someone didn’t like it, I simply didn’t care. Because in my honesty with clients, I gained a positive feeling about my role in helping families. The more I spoke honestly, the more positive an impact I began to have on people’s lives. I was a better lawyer. I became a better person, a better parent, spouse, and friend.

The firm grew. People were now attracted to our approach. I truly feel meditation had a major effect on the success of the firm. I encouraged our clients to try meditation themselves, to help find some common ground, to keep their case as civil as possible for the benefit of the children. It’s hard to give up on revenge. It’s hard to work with someone you no longer love or trust. But it is absolutely worth it if it improves your child’s life. Sales was not a focus. I focused on service, providing value, and we started to get more calls. Our numbers rose. The hard advice continued through representation.

In turn, I became more passionate about my job. And, as a positive mindset tends to do, the whole thing snowballed. I felt good going into work, I felt good about leaving my clients and coming home, I felt good about supporting my family. I was able to work towards being fully present, and pleasant, when I was with them.

Meditation single-handedly gave me the insight and curiosity to identify other powerful and life-changing tools. Six to be exact. Once I applied a new approach to law and to life, I started telling others about it, 'Tony Robbinsing' them. I feel vehement about what I learned. Life is short. Learning to navigate and experience all life has to offer is gold to me. I couldn't help but try out the Six Steps on everyone I knew, and everywhere in my life.

## Pairing Positivity with Intention

For me, meditation combines positivity with intention. Through meditation, I am able to create a positive mental atmosphere and set intentions. If I just sat in meditation and breathed about how beautiful the world is, I would be a happy person, but I probably would not be as successful as I am. Instead, I apply meditation as a productive tool rather than a relaxing escape. Meditation allows me to step back and see the whole picture for what it is. The wide array of possibilities and opportunity. The value of life itself. I can then use that reinvigorated perspective to move forward with my goals. Meditation is a tool. It isn't a beach chair.

Intention often gets a bad rap in self-help literature. It's made to sound more powerful than it actually is. If you dream it, you can achieve it. It's not that simple. Do not fool yourself into thinking you can lay on your couch and say "Ok, it is my intention to overcome type 2 diabetes." That is not enough. And this level of inaction is a block to progress.

Intention is about harnessing positive energy and using it to push forward with action. Instead of "I intend to overcome diabetes," you should be thinking, "My health is at rock bottom. If I keep overeating, I will die. I'm going to start with small changes, take things an hour at a time, do whatever it takes to overcome this self-destructive behavior." You cannot manifest yourself into curing type 2 diabetes. What you can do is get your mind right and implement small healthy steps to reducing your health risk.

Everyone responds differently to different practices. Try a few, pick what works best for you. This stuff is potent. Even five minutes a day total is enough to create significant change in your thought patterns and performance. Once you admit you are at a rock-bottom moment in your life and desperation kicks in to produce immediate action; the right frame of mind will flip your mind's response from flight mode to fight mode. And now you're on the way up.

## Remarkable Rebounds: Jim Carrey

*"I don't think human beings learn anything without desperation. Desperation is a necessary ingredient to learning anything or creating anything. Period. If you ain't desperate at some point, you ain't interesting."*[46]

Jim Carrey was a Canadian-born dyslexic child who grew up in poverty, eventually living in a van with his parents and three siblings. At fifteen, he left school, working as a janitor to help support his family. Desperate to improve their situation, he fought to launch a career in stand-up comedy. Despite failure after failure, he refused to accept defeat. He wrote himself a $10-million check and kept it in his wallet, vowing to cash it one day. In November 1995, ten years after he wrote that check, he earned $10 million for his role in *Dumb and Dumber.* His career exploded. Carrey starred in and produced many successful films, becoming a well-respected comedian with a net worth of $180 million.

---

46 Leung R. Carrey: 'Life is too beautiful.' Nov. 18, 2004. *CBS News.*

# STEP 4: MOVE

*"Movement is where change suddenly becomes visible to yourself and others."*

Once you have hit bottom, embraced desperation, and adjusted your mindset, you have created a powerful force to propel your life in new and great directions. But there are three more traits that you have to incorporate before the ball starts rolling with some force. Interestingly, through my dealings with those who rose out of trauma and adversity, all of them participated in some sort of physical activity. Some had an active job involving lots of walking and heavy lifting across the workday. Others had some hobby that involved physical movement, hiking, jogging, dancing, weight training. They all had physical movement in common. Was it just a coincidence? Or was there something about movement that contributed to their resilience and strength during severe adversity?

Humans are complex physiological beings. While we are all indeed up in our heads with our thoughts and emotions, our brain requires nutrients and good oxygen flow to function at high capacity. And the brain doesn't provide any of that. Our organ systems do. Our muscles generate heat and energy in the form of ATP. Muscle movement is the only mechanism by which our lymph is moved through the body. It is not pumped by the heart. It is pumped when we contract our muscles. Lymph is the fluid that carries antigens to the immune system. Without lymph flow, cancer cells, toxins, and infectious agents just sit there. Our heart pumps oxygen and immune cells and nutrients. Working the heart and lungs and muscle saturates the brain with every resource it needs to function. Body movement has a direct impact on brain function. And high brain function–problem solving, decision making, opportunity detecting, creativity–is critical to turning trauma into triumph.

This is basic, realistic, totally doable stuff. You don't need a gym membership. You don't have to spend an hour a day working out. It doesn't matter that you are in terrible shape. I'm not talking about running sprints. I'm talking about simple movement. Set your timer for five minutes. Do some stretches. Walk three houses down and back. Done. Stick with this for a week, a month if you want, then increase the timer to ten minutes. Add some new stuff. Do a 10-minute easy workout video online. Put on some music and walk around the block. It isn't about getting in shape. It isn't about losing weight. It is about fueling your brain.

CHAPTER 10

# ACTION GENERATES A REACTION

To move forward, you have to move. If you don't do something different, then nothing different happens. This means moving your body in some way. There is a deep link between our bodies and our minds. If you can get your body moving, it will allow you to make mental and emotional leaps you never thought you were capable of.

Shelley was a client of mine who experienced one of the worst cases of domestic abuse I've seen. Her husband was emotionally and verbally abusive towards her. He often refused to speak to her for weeks despite their children. Sometimes when she would walk up the stairs carrying one their kids, he would hip check her into the wall, bruising her body and making her fear not only for her own safety, but that of their children. When she didn't react to him, his violence would escalate, and in front of their children. My mother would have lost her shit on this 'man.'

Shelley was blinded by her situation. She couldn't acknowledge how dangerous her environment had become. She couldn't accept that she needed to get herself and her children out of there. Her situation had become her normal. It was anything but normal. It was destructive and debilitating. Domestic violence comes in all forms. Often it is emotional and psychological cruelty. It is the hardest situation to come across because, sadly, most victims aren't ready or willing to take action.

I shared with her what I've learned about the six traits of overcoming adversity and dealing with trauma. Shelley realized she was at rock bottom.

She embraced desperation. She attended domestic violence counseling for several months, started practicing meditation, and worked hard to get her mind right, much of it without her husband knowing. But it wasn't until she embraced movement that both she and I noticed the major transformations in her life.[47]

## Movement Creates Clarity

Early in the process, I recommended that Shelley find something active to do—some way to get her body moving. She didn't want to hear it. Who can blame her? She was juggling so much, just trying to survive. The thought of recreational exercise felt impossible and ridiculous. But I kept at her, told her it could be as simple as going for a walk. Maybe doing it with a friend would make it more fun.

She tried it, started walking. Then she joined a gym and started weightlifting. Going to the gym filled her brain with endorphins, gave her positive feelings. She was hooked. Suddenly, when she went home to her husband, she realized that she felt bad, sick, tired. Reality floated in. She gained clarity. Because she had found an activity that made her brain produce positive feelings, her mind suddenly was able to contrast that with the negative feelings she experienced at home. She realized how damaging her marriage was for both her and her kids.

## Movement Always Pays Off

Personally, I turn to physical activity to get me out of any difficulty. If I'm

47 Because of this case, we started providing "pre-litigation" services. Strategy sessions. Advisory services. We don't enter an appearance into the case. We help people think strategically about their case from a high level. Often this results in full-on legal representation, but it costs less because the client is prepared, well-advised, and has their mind right.

stuck on what to do at Burnham Law or in our Burnham tribe at home, I get up and move–walk, bike, swim, surf, prison workout, anything. When I've hit rock bottom with the various crises that have come into my life, forcing myself to move my body has always been the thing that triggered my climb out and up. Physical activity tricks my mind into thinking things are going great and I'm making tons of progress. I get endorphins flowing, I get into a rhythm. I start to feel, "hey, I can totally manage this thing that has exploded my world." My wife can tell when I don't work out. Movement changes me. I feel better about myself, and I gain confidence which extends to all areas of life.

Doing some form of movement every day, no matter how small, keeps me on track. My head is clearer. My sleep is better. It helps me stay in a positive mindset. It generates energy and power. Physical movement is another magic bullet, pulling me forward through the worst of times.

And, probably more often than not, I don't want to do it. Just chilling in my lounge chair with my laptop open to Netflix sounds way better. I have long conversations with myself, the angel and devil on my shoulders yapping back and forth. "I'm exhausted and dealing with hard stuff. No need to tax myself." "Listen buddy, you're going to gain serious energy and the hard stuff will look a lot less hard once you get moving." "Naw, I'll just stay here and maybe have some chips." "Just try it for two minutes. If you hate it, you can sit back down." "Woah, yeah, feels like I've had an energy shot. I can conquer the world!" "Told ya. Maybe you'll listen to me next time."

If it was easy, everyone would be doing it. But the hard part isn't the movement, the hard part is peeling yourself away from stillness. I can't name one person who *always* is raring to get up and moving, and I can't name one person who isn't glad they did.

## Action Creates Action

This book is not about physics (I'm no physicist) but we have to take a look at Newton's third law of motion: *For every action, there is an equal and opposite reaction.* Moving your body is action. The reaction is a change in your brain chemistry, which alters your mental and emotional state. Physical activity is the juice that jumpstarts your mental transformation. When you get your body moving, it gets your mind moving. And that motion is what is going to carry you forward, up and out of your rock bottom into the amazing life you are about to build. Trust me on this.

### Remarkable Rebounds: Steven Spielberg

*"I've always been very hopeful which I guess isn't strange coming from me. I don't want to call myself an optimist. I want to say that I've always been full of hope. I've never lost that."*[48]

As a child Steven Spielberg suffered from dyslexia but had a burning desire to make movies. He made short films at home and charged admission to neighbors. He applied to USC film school and was rejected three times. This was his rock-bottom moment, when it seemed he was never going to have the career he dreamed of. He moved forward and made a movie, 1941, which bombed. Another failure, but he pulled himself up again and went on to make Jaws, his first smash hit. His list of stellar movies includes ET, the Indiana Jones franchise, Saving Private Ryan, Schindler's List, The Color Purple, and many more. He is worth more than $8 billion.

---

48 McBride J. *Steven Spielberg: A Biography.* (January 4, 2011). University Press of Mississippi; 2nd ed.

CHAPTER 11

# MOVING PUTS THE PIECES TOGETHER

As human beings, we have jumped ahead of evolution. Our minds, our society, and our technology have left our bodies in the dust. We are not built to sit all day, to stare at screens, and to move only our minds. Our bodies need movement. We have not yet evolved into just being giant brains connected to networks, although we sometimes act like we are. Our brains still need body movement to function. When our bodies are moving, our minds work properly. When we move, our emotions and thought patterns function at a more optimal level.

## Movement Creates Well-Being

A 2019 study contrasted sedentary lifestyles with more active lifestyles. Sedentary lifestyles lead to a whole long list of physical problems (which has no doubt been drummed into your head already), but what you might not know is that becoming active can often undo some of the effects that a sedentary lifestyle has created. The study showed that getting your body moving delays the aging of our brains and delays or prevents diseases like Alzheimer's, diabetes, and MS.[49] The study also showed that an active lifestyle improves brain functioning and memory. Moving your body makes your brain stronger and healthier. Activity makes people happier. Physical activity creates a sense of well-being.

49 Di Liegro CM, Schiera G, Proia P, Di Liegro I. Physical Activity and Brain Health. *Genes* (Basel). 2019 Sep; 10(9): 720.

It's important to remember that although we think of our mental selves as being somehow distinct from our physical bodies, our brain is not an isolated system. For it to function, the rest of the body has to be functioning. When you exercise, your heart rate goes up. Your brain receives more oxygen, allowing it to organize and fire neurons more effectively, improving mental function. When you participate in physical activity, you increase concentration, memory, creativity, problem-solving, and emotional function.

## The Exercise Antidepressant

It might seem strange that exercise alone can make you happier, but research shows that the 'runner's high' people feel when they run is the result of new neural networks in an area of the brain called the hippocampus. Studies even suggest that exercise could be an effective antidepressant therapy all by itself.[50] Think about that. Therapy and medication have a significant effect on mental disorders. Exercise has the power to produce an equivalent effect? That seems like a deal too good to pass up. We have the ability to change the way our mind thinks and feels just by moving our bodies.

## Exercise Boosts Mood

Exercise has also been shown to improve mood.[51] Exercise increases blood circulation and influences several systems and organs in the body which results in lessened stress and improvements to anxiety and depression. In addition to the chemical effects of exercise, physical activity can also serve as a healthy form of distraction. When you're focused on playing basketball

50 Ernst C, Olson AK, Pinel JPJ. Antidepressant effects of exercise: Evidence for an adult-neurogenesis hypothesis? *J Psychiatry Neurosci.* 2006 Mar; 31(2): 84–92.

51 Sharma A, Madaan V, Petty FD. Exercise for Mental Health. Prim Care Companion *J Clin Psychiatry.* 2006; 8(2): 106.

or surfing, you aren't as cued in to your current problems. Physical activity also often includes social interaction, another activity known to improve mood. When you exercise, there is a corresponding improvement in self-esteem. Exercise convinces your brain that you're a good, useful, productive, and happy person.

## Movement Makes You Emotionally Strong

Exercise has also been shown to help your brain see and experience joy.[52] Starting new types of physical activity jumpstarts your brain to appreciate your physical abilities. You begin thinking of yourself as strong, able, and powerful. Those adjectives are spurred by the physical activity, but your brain also applies them to your mental self. You slowly start to think of yourself as emotionally resilient, mentally powerful, and strong-hearted.

This is SO important. We don't feel strong or powerful when we are steeped in trauma. When we're at the lowest point of our life, we don't see an amazing individual. When we exercise, our brain begins to tell us that we are one. It's an amazing magic trick. There you are, in the worst situation of your life. You're desperate. Nothing is looking great. You move your body, and your brain automatically changes your thoughts, showing you the truth, that you currently possess every attribute you need to change your life.

## Activity Improves Relationships

Research also shows that physical activity improves and strengthens personal

---

52 Legey S, Aquino F, Lamego MK, et al. Relationship Among Physical Activity Level, Mood and Anxiety States and Quality of Life in Physical Education Students. *Clin Pract Epidemiol Ment Health.* 2017;13:82-91.

relationships.[53] You've already read about all the ways exercise makes you happier and emotionally healthy. It makes sense that when you are happier, your relationships get better. When you are at your best, you interact with the people you care about on a higher level.

Which marriage do you think is going to be happier: a low-energy, depressed, negative-mindset, low-self-esteem couple? Or a high-functioning, creative, thoughtful, confident couple? It's a no-brainer. Of course, activity is not going to fix a broken relationship. If you're headed to divorce, physical activity probably won't fix all the things that are wrong in your marriage. Many marriage difficulties are not caused by one's mental state, just like cancer or a tragic car accident is not caused by one's mental state. But physical activity will take the divorce or cancer or car accident and process the information differently in the brain. You'll gain a different perspective. You'll be able to get through it in a healthier way with less emotional stress than if you try and navigate the adversity with a low-functioning brain, fatigued, irritable, and self-deprecating.

## Exercise Begets Bravery

Exercise gives you courage.[54] Think of all the things your body does when it exercises. It breaks through barriers, it overcomes obstacles, it moves heavy things, it builds speed, and it moves even when it starts to feel tired. Those are all descriptions of things you need to mentally be able to do to in order to beat adversity. If your body can do it, your brain starts transmitting the message that you can do it mentally and emotionally as well. This results in courage. You start to think you are brave. And brave people do hard things.

53 An HY, Chen W, Wang CW, et al. The Relationships between Physical Activity and Life Satisfaction and Happiness among Young, Middle-Aged, and Older Adults. *Int J Environ Res Public Health.* 2020;17(13):4817.

54 Anderson E, Shivakumar G. Effects of exercise and physical activity on anxiety. *Front Psychiatry.* 2013;4:27.

This gives you the armor you need to fight back against everything negative you are experiencing and gives you the strength to move forward.

Decades ago, I played collegiate lacrosse. I grew up in the hotbed that is Central New York and a ticket to college was the juice we were all after. I lifted weights, focused on strength, and I continued to do that well into my 30s even after rupturing my Achilles tendon. I'm now 50 and into my first full year of surfing. When our Kauai instructor, Kamalei, initially watched me, he could tell that I used to carry a lot of weight. I was still carrying it despite being 40 pounds lighter. He referred to me as a boulder, a large rock, on a surfboard. Doing anything for the first time isn't easy. It's uncomfortable, joining a gym, joining a rock-climbing club, joining a jogging club. It's all uncomfortable. . . unless you're desperate.

## Exercise Makes You Creative

We've talked about how desperation forces you to be creative. To really grease the wheel of creativity, you also need exercise. A report in the *New York Times* summarized some interesting studies showing that exercise makes us more creative and adaptive.[55] One study divided subjects into two groups. One was told to move around fluidly, drawing loopy, curvy lines in space with their arms. The second group was told to draw straight, angular lines in space with their arms. Then the scientists asked each group to come up with creative things to do with newspaper. The fluid movement group came up with many more creative ideas for how to use newspaper than the straight and angular movement group. The message here is that you don't have to do structured exercise. Get up and dance with your kids or chase your dog around the living room. Fun movement that feels good is much

55 Reynolds G. Can Exercise Make You More Creative? *New York Times*. Feb. 3, 2021

easier and very effective in increasing creativity, enhancing the ability to come up with innovative solutions.

Another study had one group of people sit at a desk and try to think of ways to use a button. They had a second group of people walk on a treadmill and try to think of the same thing. The walking group came up with more creative ideas than the stationary group. Movement is key. Another research project gathered information using activity trackers, seeing how active people were over a week. They then had participants come up with uses for everyday objects and to finish incomplete drawings. The more active people had more creative responses. The more regular their activity was, the more creative they were. Incorporating activity into your schedule produces big benefits. Moving your body will fuel your brain and help you find those creative, never-before-considered opportunities that will propel you up and out of your rock bottom into a better life than you had before.

## Other Benefits

Besides fueling a positive mindset and enhancing creativity, exercise is linked to numerous other lifestyle improvements. People who exercise experience:

- Better sleep
- More interest in sex
- Less stress
- Higher energy levels
- Increased stamina
- Less tiredness
- Weight loss
- Better mental alertness

Any one of those benefits alone is guaranteed to improve mood. Physical activity always pays off.

## How Much Exercise?

How much movement do we need to experience a difference in how we feel? Experts suggest that ninety total minutes of exercise per week will do the trick.[56] Seriously. An hour and a half total over a whole week. That is doable for almost anyone. You can break that up however you want. You could take nine 10-minute walks in a week. You could take one 90-minute hike a week. You could take three 30-minute bike rides. You could dance at a club for an hour and do yoga for half an hour. It doesn't matter how you do it, just that you get those 90 minutes in.

56 Depression and anxiety: Exercise eases symptoms. Sept. 27, 2017. Mayo Clinic.

## Remarkable Rebounds: Malala Yousafzai

*"I told myself, Malala, you have already faced death. This is your second life. Don't be afraid—if you are afraid, you can't move forward."*[57]

As a young girl in Pakistan, Malala Yousafzai spoke out against the Taliban ban on education for girls in her country. At age 11, her father took her to a press club where she gave a speech which was widely publicized. She was then asked to blog for the BBC about the situation, under a pseudonym. She began to do television appearances and be very public about her cause. In 2012 she was shot in the head by a Taliban gunman while returning from school in an assassination attempt. This was her rock-bottom moment. Malala survived the attack and used it to further her cause. She continues to be an outspoken advocate for women's education in suppressed societies and has won many awards, including the Nobel Prize. She has written books and formed Malala's Fund which opens schools for girls.

---

57 Yousafzai M. (October 1, 2013). *I Am Malala: The Girl Who Stood Up for Education and Was Shot by the Taliban.* Little, Brown & Co.

CHAPTER 12

# FORWARD MOTION MOVES YOU FORWARD

Remember Shelley's story? She is now divorced and free from her abusive husband. Her kids are grown and have become athletes. They mirrored her love for physical activity. She changed her children's life trajectory. She owns her own gym. She has the vast majority of parenting time. That's a nice hip check to her ex, but she doesn't waste her energy looking back. She values her time. Shelley now competes in CrossFit games. Her son is dating a CrossFit member. The physical movement she embraced not only pulled her out of rock bottom, but it also gave her kids a legacy. Our children watch us. They imitate us. If they see you living in despair, they will think that's what life is. If they see you take action, practice a positive mindset, value physical movement, and power through adversity, they will do the same. They will be attracted to versions of their parental figure. That's some serious motivation to be the best version of ourselves.

### Case Study: Malik

I emphasized the importance of physical movement with Malik. He didn't believe in its immediate and beneficial effects, but he trusted me. While he was waiting for his trial, he started watching workout videos, looking for exercises he could do with his one body weight. He built a short routine he could do on the floor and against walls, planning to continue when he was in jail.

He served his 30 days, doing some kind of exercise every single day. The time he spent building his strength helped him realize that he could handle his sentence. Exercise offered structure to his day. It became something he looked forward to. The routine he'd built served him well. When he got out, he joined a basketball league at the YMCA. He hadn't played since he was a teen, but he started playing once a week. Being active with other people only added to his enjoyment and his belief that exercise was paying off.

The feel of the ball in his hands and the rhythm of his feet on the gym floor fed his power and strength. When he left the gym, he felt he could tackle anything. As his body moved, his brain became saturated with oxygen and nutrients, feeding his positive self-image and cognitive ability.

## Physical Activity Powers Mental Strength

Shelley always had the mental strength to get out of her abusive marriage. She just didn't know it. It wasn't until physical activity gave her brain the resources it needed to function properly that she realized she was strong enough to move on with her life. When you start moving, even in small ways, your mind becomes more observant. You can clearly see the situation you are in, and the direction you need to go. If you're feeling tired, irritable, anxious, fearful, or self-conscious, just a few minutes a day of physical movement can change all of that. And you'll feel the effects that very first day.

Shelley hit bottom, embraced despair, got her mind right, but something clicked with her when she started working out. It became her purpose. Exercise gave her the drive to make change. She told me that exercise changed the entire way she felt about her life. It flipped a switch, allowed her to see where she was. And it gave her the motivation to build a new existence. When she looks back now, she says she doesn't even recognize that other version of herself. She's now living a productive life free of abuse. Physical activity was the catalyst.

## Get the Ball Rolling

What we do changes the narrative and trajectory not only of our own lives, but of the lives of those around us, especially our children. Kids watch us. Shelley's kids saw where she was and how she got out of it. They learned that if they find themselves in a bad place, they have the power to fix it. They saw that people deserve happiness and that the effort to achieve that is worth it. They saw that making small changes produced big changes. They learned it was doable. They also saw that they mattered to their mom–enough that she overcame her own fears and her own feelings of inadequacy to make a better life for them.

Step 4 is not about looking good on social media or prepping for your island vacation. You don't have to compete in anything or win approval from anyone. You don't even have to be "in shape." It's about the awakening that occurs with physical movement. It's about nourishing your brain to boost your mental clarity, vital tools when you are staging a mutiny of your own sinking ship. Believe me, I'm not a health fanatic–yet. I am slowly getting to the point where the Hershey bar doesn't taste as good as health feels, but let's think of that as my long game. I'm talking about basic movement. Movement is where change becomes viable and visible to yourself and others.

Activity is such a powerful tool. I rely on it constantly. If I'm having a tough day or struggling with something at work, I'll take a walk. If we're in

Hawaii, I'll hop on my surfboard. I've learned that moving my body moves my mind. If I cannot see a solution, I step away from the mental gymnastics and go focus on some kind of physical activity. When I come back to the problem later, it's like my mind was secretly solving it while my body was exercising. The physical motion moves my thinking forward and introduces me to solutions I couldn't see before. Physical action creates mental action.

## Do What Works

You don't have to become a gym rat to reap the benefits. You don't have to drive to a yoga studio or buy special clothes. You don't need any equipment, and you don't have to make a giant time commitment. You just have to move. Get up and walk, run, swim, bike, dance, do some sit ups. It doesn't have to be what most people think of as 'exercise.' Shake your booty while you cook. Do some jumping jacks in between work calls. Walk up and down the stairs while you wash your face. Stretch while you're watching TV. Add more the following day. More stretches, a longer jog, more stair climbs. As long as it gets you breathing heavy and gets your heart pumping.

Go back to the section on habits and use that information to help you make some kind of movement a habit in your life. Look, I have been where you are. You're in a deep, dark place, or you know someone who is. You're on the couch or in bed. You're bingeing Netflix. You've got a snack and some drinks. You have a cat on your lap or a dog next to you. You're comfy. It feels like self-care. Ben and Jerry's Phish Food is all the antidepressant you need. Getting up seems ridiculous. That would take a LOT of effort.

Yes, it does. Getting up takes a lot of effort. But it's a hell of a lot easier when you tell yourself to do just two minutes of movement and you can sit right back down. Do that. Next day, make it three minutes. No one is telling you to run a marathon. Start with a walk through the house or apartment. Do it again in a couple of hours. Look at you, you're moving! On nicer days you might want to leave the house for a walk, or maybe you want to try a 10-minute yoga stretching video on YouTube. Keep things new. Try different types of movement. Tell yourself it's just an experiment. If you don't like it, you never have to do it again. Notice how your thoughts change. You can do this!

## Biggest Loser

One of my favorite television shows is The Biggest Loser. Obese people come on a TV show, learn how to work out and eat right, and lose hundreds of pounds. Hundreds of pounds. Gone. Life transformed. Unless, that is, the old habits come back. You must keep stacking bricks. Sometimes that means trying new things.

As a former competitive college athlete, my body has been pretty banged up. Even after losing the 30 pounds, my body was still stiff. I used to have chronic back pain, which has lessened, but it is still there. In every step, there is a deeper step if you want to go deeper. As I transformed my body in my late 40s, my weaknesses rose to the top. Lack of flexibility in the hips, hamstring tightness, and Achilles soreness were the norm.

One day I spoke with my college friend, Derek, and he told me about his podcast called Guys Talking Yoga. He was like an infomercial for the practice of yoga, outlining all I knew to be true, and that has become a new practice for me. His passion for the topic oozed from him, and I knew right away that I was about to go full-crunchy and start a yoga practice.

So, now I meditate and practice yoga while still incorporating weight training. Adversity started this search. Everyone's journey is different.

## Remarkable Rebounds: Michael Jordan

*"Always turn a negative situation into a positive situation."*[58]

As a teen, Michael Jordan tried out for his high school varsity basketball team. He didn't make the cut. This was his rock bottom because basketball was his dream, his only goal. He refused to give up and practiced harder. Whenever he felt like giving up, he visualized the team list without his name on it. It motivated him to keep going. After practicing nonstop and growing four inches, he made the team as a junior. He did so well that he was named a McDonald's All American. He made the team at UNC Chapel Hill. He won gold in the Olympics. Jordan went on to become one of the greatest players in NBA history. He received the Presidential Medal of Freedom and built a giant endorsement empire.

---

58 Jordan M. (2005). *Driven From Within.* Atria; First Ed.

## STEP 5: STACK BRICKS

*"To maintain momentum, you must home in on the trees. Forget the forest."*

There is a fifth trait that people who thrive after severe adversity have in common. In addition to admitting they've hit rock bottom, embracing desperation, getting their mind right, and moving, these superhumans know how to stack bricks.

When you are at rock bottom, you look up at that goal you want to achieve. It's all the way up on the peak of a mountain. From where you're at, it seems completely impossible that you could ever climb that high. You're tired. You're hurt. You're disturbed by where you've ended up. How can you even begin to garner the level of motivation it will take to get up there? For a start, stop looking at the big picture problem.

Rather than focusing on getting to the top of that mountain, reaching your goal, focus on standing up. Once you've done that, focus on taking one step forward. And once that is done, focus on the next step. We rebuild our lives one brick at a time. Constructing a skyscraper seems like a massive task. But that is an illusion. In reality, all you have to do is place one brick. Then the next. Then the next. Don't step back and survey your progress every three bricks. Just keep focusing on each individual brick. At the end of the day, you can see where you're at. But one brick at a time is the key. Stop looking for big wins. Small wins are just as fruitful. Getting out of bed is a win. Taking a shower is a win. Each is a brick added to the new life you are building.

CHAPTER 13

# SMALL WINS TOTAL UP TO BIG WINS

Jerry was a client of ours who survived a near-fatal auto accident. His car was T-boned by a commercial truck. He nearly died, found himself in the hospital with a dislocated hip, two torn ligaments in his legs, and a broken knee-cap. He couldn't walk normally even after he got through the surgeries and the initial physical therapy. In addition to his pain and disability, his injury meant he wouldn't be able to get affordable health insurance. Now he had a pre-existing condition. He couldn't work again, couldn't earn an income, and the medical bills were already piling up. Jerry had hit rock bottom.

We took Jerry's case. We worked to ensure that Jerry won a huge settlement. We wanted to make sure he would be taken care of for the rest of his life. The insurance company, not surprisingly, didn't want to pay him a dime. We did not rest until we were able to hand him that giant check. When I gave it to him and said, "Congratulations! We did it!" I felt fantastic. But Jerry was just pissed off.

He said, "Todd, I'm 30 years old. I'm never going to walk normally again. For the rest of my life, this is going to be my reality. I can't work. I can't take a shower without help. I have three kids and a wife. This money doesn't fix anything." In fact, no amount of money is enough to "fix" circumstances like Jerry's. Life as he knew it was over. You can't buy it back.

Jerry was pissed that this happened to him, pissed that at age 30 insurance companies deemed him permanently disabled, pissed that the insurance company made us sue them and go through a long, drawn-out case to get the money he rightfully deserved from the start. He was furious that the guys in suits who put him through all those legal hurdles could now just hand over a check that they KNEW they were going to have hand over at the beginning (but they fought it anyhow) and just walk away and get on with their merry lives. The whole thing was over for them. It would never be over for Jerry.

The money at least meant he could pay his mortgage and get the health care he needed, but he wanted more. He deserved more. And he was determined to get it.

## The Art of Brick Laying

Jerry knows how to stack bricks. Jerry took that insurance check and started doing the largest amount of physical rehab his therapist allowed. This was his revenge. He was going to turn out better than before just to show those assholes what he was made of. He made huge strides in his recovery. I asked him how he found the motivation and drive to do it. He said, "I'm just stacking bricks."

Jerry explained his plan to me. He said, "Every day, I have a choice. I can either stack more bricks towards the life I want to achieve, or I can use the same amount of time, effort, and energy to remove bricks. Given those two choices, I'm going to stack bricks every efing day until I get to where I want to be."

Jerry had a goal, and sitting around moaning about how far away that goal was would not get him there. He intuitively knew that small, individual steps were the means to the end, stacking one brick on top of another.

## Small Victories Accumulate

Jerry's approach was entirely new to me. Jerry's plan was to collect small wins. Every time he got out of bed was a brick. Every time he went to physical therapy was a brick. Every time he made a slight improvement in his physical ability, he recognized it as a win and added it to the structure he was creating. Jerry homed in on the small wins. He aimed only for one small piece of progress at a time. When he achieved it, he had reached his ultimate goal. Because the only goal in front of him was placing the next brick. Each step forward boosted his confidence. He was getting somewhere. He was capable of moving forward. He didn't expect to recover in a couple of weeks, or months, or even a year. He didn't care when he got there. All he cared about was that next brick.

It was genius. Instead of pressuring himself to completely recover and run a marathon, Jerry worked for a single improvement at a time. He was achieving multiple goals a day. He didn't get up and say to himself, "I want to be able to go rock climbing." He said to himself, "I want to do five more reps of that new exercise." Because the goals were small, he was constantly achieving things. He almost never set a goal he couldn't meet. Yeah, some days were harder than others, but in general each thing he asked himself to do was possible. And when he achieved it, he felt awesome and strong, racking up another medal on that mental chart. He was a constant winner.

## Trauma Is Not an Olympic Sport

The thing I love about Jerry's story is, he's a real guy who was in a really terrible spot. A lot of the time when you hear about motivation and achievement it's always about Olympic athletes and CEOs and how they achieve amazing things. Yay for them, but try learning how to walk again after a truck mows you down. . . THAT takes motivation and strength. Try learning to go out on a date with a new person after you've been raped. Try being able to build a productive, happy life after your child dies of a brain tumor. Try being able to live a normal life after you've gone to rehab, been homeless, lost custody of your kids, been to jail, or lost everything at the blackjack table. Try going through a nasty divorce or getting sued for millions of dollars, or being charged with a crime as you are escorted from your workplace in handcuffs. It isn't the Olympic athletes and CEOs that impress me. I want to learn from survivors.

Coming back from trauma takes fortitude, bravery, and mental toughness. Just putting on your shoes after trauma, then building on one tiny piece at a time, to eventually end up living your absolute best life ever is heroic and amazing. Jerry showed me the secret ingredient: the stacking bricks mindset. It made sense to me as I understand the 'one day at a time' concept. But bricks are heavy. It gives weight (a brick) to actions. I survived one day at a time, but I stacked a ton of bricks.

Jerry's approach circumvents fear. If you step back and take a look at the big picture, it's easy to become overwhelmed with fear. What if I fail? What if I can't get there? That kind of anticipatory dread and doubt can be paralyzing. If odds are you're just going to fail anyhow, why even try? But with Jerry's method there is no fear of failure. Challenging yourself to go to a counseling appointment or to do one hour of your court-ordered community service is a cinch. There's almost zero risk of failure. When you set goals you can't fail at, you are guaranteed success. FEAR, again, is simply False Evidence Appearing Real.

## Bird By Bird

There's a well-known writer, Anne Lamott, who tells a story in one of her books about her brother. When she and her brother were kids, her brother had to write a report for school about birds. He kept putting it off. He couldn't sit down at the kitchen table and write that report. He couldn't even start it. It seemed like a completely insurmountable task to write down everything he had learned about birds.

Finally, their dad told him he just needed to go bird by bird. Just write about one bird. When you're done, write about another one. Anne's brother no longer had to write some massive report. He just had to write what he knew about owls. Then what he knew about hawks. Then what he knew about sparrows. The report itself was overwhelming, but once he broke it down into pieces it became completely doable. It's the same with life. Bird by bird, brick by brick. Focus on one single step. Don't even think about the next one until you are done with the first. And don't let yourself look at the big picture. You'll be there soon enough.

## Chunking

This is also the concept behind the time management strategy called chunking. If you're at work one day and have twenty things to do on your schedule, you can end up accomplishing almost nothing. You jump from phone call to email to meeting to Zoom to a spreadsheet. By the end of the day, you look at the remaining fifteen tasks you have yet to do and just decide to skip out early. It's impossible. Might as well try again tomorrow.

Those savvy in time management know how to get every task done. By chunking. Say you have an eight-hour workday. Divide those eight hours into 15-minute increments. Set your timer for 15-minutes, then focus on a single task during that 15-minute block. Put your phone in a drawer, close your email program, and complete that task. Now set your time again and take the next 15 minutes to answer emails. Then set up a time to respond to voicemail. Stop trying to multitask, breaking your job down into small manageable, focused pieces, and watch how much you accomplish.

Brick laying is the same concept. You can't build a new life in a day. But if you make a list of small, easy tasks, or "bricks," and set aside a block of time to focus on a single task, you will make real, valuable progress. Don't focus on your list. Pick a task, put the list away, and focus.

## Climbing Mount Everest

Eight hundred people a year make the climb to the summit of Mount Everest. Up on Everest, at the cruising altitude of a passenger jet, the atmosphere is thin. There is not enough oxygen to support life. Most can't make the climb without an oxygen tank, and even with supplemental oxygen it takes eight to ten hours to climb just 3,000 feet. You do not reach the top of Mount Everest by focusing on the summit. You get to the top by focusing on your next step. For this reason, thousands of folks become addicted to the climb. They want to try it over and over. That extreme level of focus is freeing, a form of meditation, where the mind is focused solely on one simple task, that next step.

If you know, you know. Setting small, achievable goals and celebrating each individual win is a way of life. Stacking bricks works. The technique will get you anywhere you want to go, no matter how impossible it seems. A single brick is the only goal you should be focusing on. A single win. To maintain momentum, you must home in on the trees. Forget the forest. It shows up.

## Remarkable Rebounds: Gabrielle Union

*"I had to hit rock bottom, I had to lose everything. For me that was my first marriage, going through the divorce process. I lost my show, my show was canceled. And I was having difficult relationships with my BFFs."*[59]

After dropping out of high school, actress Gabrielle Union was working at a Payless shoe store when the store was robbed. She was sexually assaulted and beaten. She survived but developed PTSD from the experience. She became an advocate, speaking to victims of assault. She went to college and became a model. She eventually began acting on television shows and then in films including *Bring It On* and *The Birth of a Nation.* In 2006, she divorced NFL player Chris Howard and hit rock bottom. In addition to the sexual assault and the end of her marriage, she experienced a variety of career failures. "It just felt like every so many years, there was some major catastrophic event that was happening in my life. You know, divorce, career setbacks, relationship issues. There's always something that just lands you on your ass and you're like 'There's no way I can move on from this, I'll never recover, I'll never be the same.'" She characterizes each setback as a mini death that she had to come back from.

---

59 Red Table Talk – Girls Trippin' with Gabrielle Union. Facebook series. May 28, 2018.

CHAPTER 14

# THE PROGRESS PRINCIPLE

The idea of taking small steps and building one tiny success on another is well-established. I love the visual form of Jerry's take on it. Stacking bricks feels concrete and productive. Stacking bricks generates a solid structure. No wolf is going to huff and puff and blow your house down. Brick buildings have staying power.

Stacking bricks made sense to me. You're wiped out by tragedy in your life, paralyzed by seemingly insurmountable obstacles. You can barely even get through the day. Forget about the day. Don't even think about the next hour. Just pick something to do right this minute and focus on that. Brush your teeth. Brick. Load the dishwasher. Brick. Put gas in your car. That's a big brick because I hate putting gas in the car. Sweet. The successes just keep stacking up and each one makes you feel. . . better. Accomplished.

Stacking bricks isn't about doing hard things. Bricks are small, simple tasks. But some tasks are bricks, they contribute to growth and make progress toward the final structure, and some tasks smash bricks, remove them. Just ask yourself when you begin to focus on a new task, whether that task is contributing to your structure or subtracting from it. Tasks that make no impact at all (like drinking a bottle of wine or spending four hours playing Call of Duty) consume the same time and energy as tasks that make an impact. That time and energy cannot be replaced.

Spend your time and energy on bricks–any task you want, as long as it contributes to your new life in some small way. Maybe when you sit down for some Netflix tonight you decide to watch a documentary or an inspirational biography instead of an action flick or comedy. Sure, watching a comedy makes us temporarily happy, and happiness is a good thing. But watching a biography of a real person who overcame real obstacles can have a powerful impact. You'll find yourself thinking about it the next day.

When we're facing adversity, any setback can send us spiraling, certain that the ultimate goal is unattainable. But setting small, attainable goals compounds your successes. One day you'll wake up and find yourself halfway up that mountain. It's a shocker, I'm telling you.

## Meaningful Goals

A *Harvard Business Review* study took a look at what gave people motivation to continue working.[60] The study analyzed bad days and good days at work. It found that 76 percent of good days were days where the respondents had made progress. Even small bits of progress produced positive results and helped people feel good about their day. The size or amount of the progress didn't matter. What mattered was, they observed forward movement.

The study also showed that while progress was important, it also mattered that the progress was meaningful in some way, even if it was a small way. If you accomplish a task that has no impact on your ultimate goal, it's not meaningful. It's not forward movement. But any progress that contributes in some small way to your goal will have a significant impact.

If your ultimate goal is to repair the relationship with your child that was severely damaged when you became addicted to painkillers, the bricks you choose to stack should have some small relationship to that ultimate goal. Your bricks might include texting your child every day even if there

60 Amabile TM, Kramer SJ. (May 2011). The Power of Small Wins. *Harvard Business Review.*

is no response, going to rehab meetings, taking a walk when you feel overwhelmed. Those tasks are good bricks. They contribute to the end structure, the ultimate goal. Don't fool yourself into thinking that going to a bar with a friend, lying in bed watching TikTok, or binging The Bachelor episodes are bricks, because they aren't. They absorb the same amount of time and energy as bricks, but there is negative progress. Zero payoff.

Bricks should be small and achievable. If Jerry challenges himself to do five more step-ups at physical therapy, that seems like a small challenge, but it is inching him toward his goal of being able to walk without pain. A very important brick. If Jerry set aside five minutes a day to snack on Reese's peanut butter cups, that's five minutes a day wasted. And when you are at your rock bottom, desperate to get out, starving, drowning, wasting five minutes is huge. Unimaginable. Choose small bricks and make sure that they contribute to your ultimate goal in some small way.

## Progress Perpetuates Itself

Another important concept that same study revealed is something called the progress loop. Once a person starts making progress, it internally motivates them to keep on making progress–inertia (more physics). An object in motion stays in motion. The feeling of progress is addictive. We want to experience it again and again. We take more steps and achieve more progress. The key lies in small wins. Wins fuel motivation. Even the smallest accomplishments power the urge for progress. Once you get it moving, it takes on a life of its own, building more and more progress.

One of the reasons the brick idea works is because it presents small, easily achievable goals. There are lots of books out there designed to help people become successful and achieve goals. Almost all of them break things down into stages. Identify your goal, define it specifically, then DO it. The problem with this is that almost everyone jumps in all gung-ho, takes a couple of big actions, falls on their face, hits a wall, and then thinks, "Well, I'll never do that again. Guess I'm not cut out for it." They are focused on that big goal on the forest. They make no wins, no progress, see no success, and decide the whole thing is ridiculous.

By stacking bricks, you rarely experience failure. And because you are never looking at the big picture, only the next step in front of you, you don't even see how far you've travelled. By the time you look up, you are halfway there. If you don't accomplish a small task, the task was too big. Start smaller. A brick isn't getting a job. A brick is revising your resume or filling out three job applications a day.

### Example: Weight Loss Bricks

If your ultimate goal is to lose 40 pounds, recognize it, then shut it away in a closet and don't think of it again. Just start stacking bricks. You lay a brick each time you open the fridge door and choose to make a turkey sandwich instead of eating a slice of pie. Win. Too hard? Then stack a brick by getting a big garbage bag and tossing out every unhealthy item from the kitchen. Get rid of it. Now you won't have to make the choice. A big win. You lay a brick when you put blueberries in your shopping cart and bypass the cookie isle. Who cares why you did it? You just did it. Another win. You lay a brick when you suddenly feel hungry and decide to drink a full glass of water, vacuum the living room, play a quick phone game, or play with the dog (we misinterpret boredom and thirst as hunger 50 percent of the time).

Think outside the box when choosing bricks. For example, get rid of your scale–choose to never weigh yourself again. Pounds are no longer the issue.

Only stacking bricks. In many cases, the extra weight on our bodies makes us feel 'safe.' It's a defense mechanism. Seeing a loss of a few pounds on the scale subconsciously 'frightens' us into eating again. Our defenses trick us, telling us, "Wow, you've got this weight loss thing down! You can have a cupcake. It won't hurt." So, get rid of that bathroom scale. Another brick, another win.

A brick is each tiny move you make toward your ultimate goal–which you are no longer focused on. You are only focused on stacking bricks. Anytime you fail at stacking a brick, adjust something to make it easier (emptying the fridge of unhealthy foods versus having to make a choice between foods).

## Perceive Progress

Building momentum by stacking bricks makes hitting an ultimate goal incredibly easy, but only if you make a point to identify *and* reward yourself for your small wins. Each brick you stack is obviously a win. But many people are resistant to accepting that fact. It can be hard to feel confident that a tiny brick is worth anything at all. And those that surround us certainly aren't handing out trophies every time we put blueberries in our shopping cart.

Why is it so hard to be proud of small wins? It's that big picture thing again. "In the big scheme of things, revising my resume or cleaning out my fridge doesn't even matter." Stay *away* from the big picture. Focus on the trees, not the forest. The big picture is too overwhelming, too impossible to comprehend. Those who have accomplished great things throughout history weren't looking to accomplish great things. They were too busy working on tiny projects. Carefully examining the details of each tree instead of trying to comprehend some infinite forest.

The perception in our society is that we have to dream BIG to win.

"Go big or go home!" That's bullshit. We get excited about champions, billionaires, and watching other people on television live their lives, hoping we were doing something else. But those folks didn't sit on the couch. They became who they are by stacking bricks. We don't hear about the millions of small wins it took to reach success. We just hear about the end success. A skyscraper isn't just plopped down in New York City as one big object. It is made of many tiny parts. The skyscraper is just the end result of innumerable bolts. And those bolts didn't get placed by waving some magic wand.

Make a point to cherish each brick, see it for what it is. Because each small win IS the progress–not the end result. High-five yourself in the air. Put a smile on your face. Recognize each win. Feel it. Embrace it. You sat in the sun for 10 minutes today after hiding in the house for a couple of weeks? That's progress! Congratulate yourself! "Geez, I'm such a badass!" You must come to truly adore each brick you stack.

## The Importance of Rewards

It can be hard to believe your small steps are real wins. So, find ways to reward yourself, to highlight that progress as a win. If you're struggling with this, there are a couple of ways to make it real. Make a sticker chart. Write down three bricks for the day and stick a gold star on it once it's done. No, we aren't in kindergarten. But the physical act of sticking that star helps imprint your brain with the feeling of reward. It also serves as a visual reminder of your success throughout the day.

Buy something cool in bulk, something collectable, polished rocks or small fossils or marbles or mahjong tiles. Put them away and take one out each time you stack a brick. Display them on an end table. Buy a Lego Death Star kit or a difficult-level model car and add to the build each time you stack a brick. Too much? Just keep a notepad near you and write down each brick. Not only are you rewarding yourself for each win, but you are able to visualize your progress in a concrete way, building momentum that propels you toward your future.

A study in *The Journal of Personality and Social Psychology* found that rewards are not only important when you complete a task, but it is also important to collect rewards throughout the process.[61] Immediate rewards just for working on a task (without completing it) increased participants' interest and enjoyment of the task. Working on the task itself becomes rewarding, rather than accomplishing the task. Let's say you are recovering from compulsive hoarding disorder and one of the bricks is to sort through the mail every day and throw out things you don't need. When you bring in the mail, reward yourself. When you sort it into piles on the table, reward yourself. When you file important statements, reward yourself. And when you throw out the pieces you don't need, another reward. Rewarding the process of brick stacking is just as effective as rewarding each stacked brick–and makes it all the more fun.

61 Hur, J. D., & Nordgren, L. F. (2016). Paying for performance Performance incentives increase desire for the reward object. *J. Pers. Soc. Psychol,* 111(3), 301–316

## Remarkable Rebounds: Chen Zhou

*"Everyone gets knocked down in life. The winners get up no matter how many times they get knocked down."*[62]

Chen Zhou is a Chinese citizen who lost both legs in a train accident at age 13. This was his rock bottom. What kind of a future could he have with no legs in rural China? He found any work he could to survive after the accident, including singing in the streets. Zhou climbs mountains using only his hands and two wooden blocks he calls shoes for his hands. He has climbed all of China's Five Great Mountains as well as the 7200 steps to the top of Mount Tai 11 times. He married his wife at the summit during one of the climbs. Zhou travels China giving street concerts and is hailed as a hero.

62 Zhou C. (204, July). The Meaningful Life Without Legs [Video]. TEDxHKBU TED Conferences. https://youtu.be/iivZL8cf7y8

CHAPTER 15

# FOCUS ON THE SHORT VIEW

Today Jerry is physically stronger than he was before the accident. Take a minute to let that sink in. Jerry, who could not walk without pain, is now *stronger* than he was before the accident. He was certain he would never walk normally again, and he's better today than he was the day before his accident. He does Ironman competitions. He got his body to where he wanted it to be which was better than before the accident. And because of the accident and the settlement, he has a nest egg for his kids. He is living a life that is better than what he had before his life fell apart. The trauma he went through brought him to where he is today. He says that getting hit by that truck was the best thing that ever happened to him. He came back better.

## Case Study: Malik

Malik had hit rock bottom, embraced his desperation, built a positive mindset, and got his body moving, nourishing his mind. When he got out of jail, he was in a great position to rebuild and begin his comeback. There was nothing easy about it, though. Despite his positive attitude, Malik had a mountain to climb. But he knew the Six Steps. And instead of getting overwhelmed and falling back into his old habits, Malik started stacking bricks.

The first problem was that his savings were nearly gone. He needed money to pay for culinary school, but he had to find a way pay for it. He defined his ultimate goal, then locked it away and focused on identifying small bricks he could stack. Malik got a job working construction. The pay was good. It was physical work which kept him moving. He started to save money bit by bit, brick by brick. He invited his cousin to continue to live with him, asking for a few hundred dollars in rent plus ongoing help with his dad. Malik went to the library each week and checked out different cookbooks, building his background and knowledge about food. Each dish was a brick. Each one was important. Each one was a vital part of the end success, but he wasn't looking at the end. He stayed steady and stacked them one by one.

He identified other bricks. His drinking habit was taking up a big chunk of his time. He wasn't in a place that required treatment, drinking up to three nights a week, but he knew his drinking was not doing him any favors. He never once woke up thinking, "Wow, I'm so thankful I drank that sixer last night." He'd had an amazing 30 days of sobriety during his jail time. Why ruin it? He decided to stop, replacing his drinking buddies with basketball at the YMCA, social media culinary groups, and cooking at home. Three solid bricks.

Malik's dad suddenly passed away at home. He never had to go to a nursing home. Malik knew he'd given him good final years. He'd succeeded despite seemingly impossible circumstances. Within two years, Malik had his tuition money. He stacked more bricks by applying to schools. He got in at New York state and moved out there, taking a part-time job at a hydroponic farm to pay his expenses, adding knowledge to his farm-to-table approach. Today Malik is the head chef of a restaurant in Boulder, Colorado. Before he knew it, he'd stacked so many bricks he was living his dream.

Malik had patience. There was no immediate success for him. It took patience and perseverance to achieve his dreams and change his life. He didn't let himself get overwhelmed. Instead, he took action every single day to move forward. He told me that sometimes it was hard to be patient, but as he saw his tuition money starting to build in his bank account, he recognized each deposited check as a success and it motivated him to keep going.

## Short Game, Long Game

What I love about Jerry's story is that it's nothing like the typical inspirational story. Self-help books are full of stories about guys who lived in their mom's basement and then started a company and made a million dollars, or women who lost 100 pounds and sold a patent for an energy supplement and married the Ken doll of their dreams. Success stories are rarely about people who had their lives completely explode to the point where they had lost all semblance of hope, and then ended up building a life better than before.

Jerry's story isn't about how he built a business or sold something or created some groundbreaking product. Jerry created change within himself. He physically changed his body through his own sheer will and determination. He transformed the deepest darkest part of his life into a secure, healthy, positive place. His success story is the change he made in his own life with his own will.

Jerry did this one brick at a time. Anyone in any situation can achieve their ultimate goal, but only One. Brick. At. A. Time. You cannot go into this certain that you will transform your life in eight weeks. You can't just manifest a massive change in your life by visualizing it either. This is about setting bricks. Focusing on one brick at a time. Do not get ahead of yourself, and start to plan your bricks. Figure out only the very next brick. Lay that brick and have a mini celebration. Then you can think about the next brick.

This is incredibly important. All the big planners out there are going to want to make some calendar of bricks they will stack this month. But if you try to define all your future bricks, bad things happen. First, you have no idea what opportunities are going to present themselves tomorrow. Your whole brick schedule would then need to be changed. It's too overwhelming, and a time waster. Time is your most valuable resource. Second, looking at a big list of bricks is going to feel too overwhelming. It's the same thing as ignoring the trees and trying to see the forest. It will only derail your motivation.

Instead, what one small task can you do right this minute? Focus on that one small task, get it done. Now you can come up with the next brick, but only after you have finished the first. Don't let yourself stare at that big goal. Remember we put it in a closet? It has to stay there. Do not engage with it. You are about your step for this moment and that is it. Maybe tomorrow you will want to do two bricks. Maybe not. Figure that out when you get there.

## Aim Low

When choosing your bricks, I'm going to tell you to do opposite of what every other self-help voice on this planet will say. I am not going to tell you to aim high, to stretch, to challenge yourself. Nope. I'm here to tell you to aim low. Very low. Nothing is going to throw you off track faster than "shooting for the stars." Keep it simple. Very simple.

My client Ana was the victim of a sexual assault perpetrated by someone she thought was a friend. It was intensely traumatic, incredibly damaging, and emotionally painful. The assault made her afraid to leave home and built up intense, crippling social anxiety. She did not feel safe being in public or in any social gathering. If you had told Ana, "Aim high girl! Be strong and go to a concert!" Ana would have simply felt "abnormal," a failure, and retreated even further. Big steps were not possible for her in any way.

Instead, Ana started with incremental exposure therapy. A small brick. She started by simply opening her front door and standing in it every day for a week. Each day was a win. Her next brick was to stand on the porch. That was a big step for her. She then got down the walkway. She built these bricks, one on top of the other until she was one day able to go into a grocery store. She didn't buy anything–she walked in, paused, and left. But that was a gigantic achievement for her. Ana kept at it, compiling her small goals and eventually, with the help of her therapist, she was able to resume normal activities AND start a successful career as a pharmaceutical sales rep, going in person to doctor's offices to make sales. It took months and months, and many bricks. Ana didn't get there by aiming to become a pharmaceutical sales rep. She would've laughed you out of the room if you even suggested such a possibility. She only got there by taking small actions that did not scare or overwhelm her, or seem impossible. Each win boosted her momentum.

When you have hit your personal apocalypse, you can't expect to pull yourself all the way out and back to normal life. Your 'normal' is forever gone. If that is your goal for today, you will fail. You cannot go from here to there. It's impossible. What you can do is begin small. When your small wins accumulate, you'll be amazed. Aim small, miss small. Aim big, miss big.

## Choosing Your Bricks

I would love to tell you that you've got time to sit back and discuss options and strategies with your best friend, sleep on the possibilities, take long walks and contemplate which steps you should take and all the pros and cons of each. But this isn't a dress rehearsal. It isn't a movie. We get one life. Money is replaceable, things are replaceable, but time is not replaceable. If you are in a place of desperation, you have to act, not think.

Certain bricks must be stacked before others. You have to lay the foundation before adding the walls. Stack the bricks that are directly in front of you first. This will help you build momentum. Getting out of bed is a brick. Taking a shower is a brick. When you are in a difficult situation, these may be your very first challenges. And it's OK, because those bricks are critical to the final product. Clean your home. Do dishes. Get organized in your space so your mind isn't cluttered. I come back to that a lot.

There may come a time where you're not sure what the next bricks should be. You might feel stumped. Even though you're desperate enough to throw anything against the wall to see if it sticks, you might have difficulty finding something you can pick up and throw.

In that situation, there are several ways to get those bricks to materialize before your eyes:

1. **Brainstorm**. What do you want to do right this minute? Does that thing move you forward in some way? You may not feel like getting up and decluttering your house. But could you pull a trash can over to the bed and clean out your bedside drawer while listening to a podcast? Do it. You may not feel like going for a walk outside, but how about a quick five-minute yoga video on the bedroom floor? There are millions of opportunities to advance. Brainstorming what

you *feel* like doing rather than what you feel you *should* be doing can help. Somewhere in there you'll find a tiny nugget or idea that is your next brick.

2. **Talk.** Previously I suggested that it is helpful to have other people in your life who are on similar journeys. Call those people and talk to them. Ask them to take a walk with you (kill two birds with one stone–physical movement and brick stacking). Tell them you feel stuck. Ask them what they do when they feel stuck. What would they do if they were you? Tell them your ideas. Ask for feedback. Most likely than not, you're going to come away from that session with a small brick you can stack. And once you get that one brick stacked, you'll find it easier to come up with the next one. Conversations with a friend can spark ideas.

3. **Inventory the bricks you've already stacked.** Looking back at what you've already achieved will get your mind moving in the flow of progress again. It's like a spinning wheel–once it starts, it wants to just keep spinning. Get it started by reminding yourself of all the tiny bricks you've already stacked. If you feel like you haven't accomplished jack squat, let me remind you that you picked up this book and that alone qualifies as a nice sized brick.

4. **Open your eyes and ears.** Read, web surf, listen to podcasts, watch TV, listen to music, Google stupid things, flip through social media groups related to your ultimate goal. Progress does not occur in a vacuum, and neither does creativity. Ideas come from observing the world around us. You can be targeted in what you do (listen to

podcasts about wellness if you are fighting back from a stroke) or you can just be free and loose, adventurous, looking for inspiration or ideas anywhere. You aren't going to get new perspectives sitting still and recounting all your mistakes. See, hear, and interact with the world, and you will find something you can do to move forward.

5. **Ask your brain for help.** When I am absolutely stuck on a work problem, I ask my brain for help before I go to bed. The whole point of sleep is to sort and file all the data we collected throughout the day. To "defragment" the hard drive, integrate the new information, and organize it into an accessible form. During sleep, our brains compute answers to the questions we presented it with during the day. I harness that property by giving my brain an assignment. More often than not, the next day, an innovative solution just pops into mind. Before you go to bed, think to yourself "Tricia, listen. I'm going to need some good bricks tomorrow. Figure it out and let me know." Leave it at that. Go to bed. There's a good chance that the next day you're going to come up with some good stuff.

## Have Patience

The Six Steps are not a get-rich-quick approach. None of this is about transforming your life in a week or a month, or even a year. The tortoise wins the race, not the hare. You must be in it for the long game. Remember that your success is going to compound, just like interest does. If you put $1,000 in the bank, you will earn $10 in interest. In year two, you are earning interest on $1,010. And so on and so on. You earn interest on the interest. When you set small goals, they are going to start to compound on each other. The more you achieve, the more powerful each achievement becomes.

Who wouldn't love to win the lottery and have everything perfect tomorrow? But the game of life doesn't work that way. Life is the journey itself, not the end. We don't take a U-Haul with us to the grave packed with all the stuff we've amassed. So slow down. Enjoy the ride, even when it's treacherous and rocky. Take your eyes away from the end goal and celebrate each small victory. Find satisfaction in each achievement and you will find that you develop patience. Look at the long game.

## Stop Judging Yourself

If you have a tough inner critic, you might find that critic has some particularly harsh words about the bricks you're stacking. "ANYONE can make a phone call. Who the eff cares? That's not progress." "Earning $25 by doing one Instacart shop is not going to solve your financial problems."

Listen, the inner critic is a child, a toddler in a toy store throwing a tantrum because you won't give it what it wants right this minute. Tell the critic to settle down, relax, chill. Put it in a timeout. We aren't solving this problem today. We aren't even attempting to solve it today. All we are doing is taking action and moving forward. Bricks are small. They are not hard. You are fulfilling the mission by taking small, accessible positive steps. That is winning.

Suspend judgment of your progress and of yourself. Like you would a child, you can listen to your inner critic's concerns, but then explain to the critic that "we aren't doing things the way you want. We are doing things the right way. So, settle down." You now live in a judgment-free zone. Every step you take is valuable. You are a champion just by showing up. Every bit of progress is a massive victory. Keep your mind right.

## Develop Momentum

Your biggest challenge is to stay out of the way as your snowball becomes an avalanche. You need desperation and a positive mindset to get it rolling, but once it starts to move, do not stand in front of it and slow it down. Step aside and let the momentum carry you. Go with the flow of the progress you make. Let it form a rip tide that pulls you along.

Trust in yourself. Understand clearly that the bricks you are laying are building your future. The foundation, the walls, the bay windows, the indoor pool. Once you start, it's easy to keep going. You've proven you can move forward, and an object in motion stays in motion.

There are several things that will try and erect a big wall to stop your progress avalanche.

- **Fear.** You may be afraid that this isn't going to work or that you will ultimately fail. It would be so much easier to sit back and do five shots of whisky. But remember this, if you feel afraid, refer back to desperation. A starving person is not afraid of eating a grubworm. A drowning person will cling to their worst enemy if it means getting out of the water. Without desperation, we wouldn't even consider doing these things. Desperation banishes fear. How desperate are you?

- **Criticism.** True support is rare. Many people in your life might look down their nose at what you're achieving, often out of jealousy or regret for their own inability to leap ahead. They may try to convince you that you're not really getting anywhere, that you should just accept things as they are, have a beer. Like your inner critic, these non-supporters are children. They feel uncomfortable and are retaliating. Tell them to chill, or stop listening. There are billions of folks on social media who have inspirational, supportive, productive things to say. Make new friends that are doing great things and will help keep the ball rolling.

- **Exhaustion.** Trauma is debilitating. The body and mind shut down. Fatigue is a common symptom of trauma. So, lean on the positive mindset, physical motion, and bricklaying. They have the remarkable tendency to kill exhaustion. Trust them. The debilitating fatigue will gradually dissipate as small wins generate energy.

- **Indecision.** If you don't know what to do next to keep moving forward, leverage your desperation. You're in a small room with no clear exit. Bang on the walls, kick at the door, bust open a window. Don't aim, just fire. There are no decisions. There is only effort. Any effort helps.

## Get in the Rhythm

Remember that last step where we learned the importance of physical movement to mental function? Here's where we tie that into the bricklaying. Think about what it feels like when you walk. You have to make yourself get up and go, but once you start moving, your feet just keep going. One after the other. Step, step, step. You just feed a little energy into it to keep moving. To stop walking, though, you have to break that rhythm. You have to interfere with the repetition. The progress you will make with stacking your bricks is similar. Lifting that first one requires some convincing, but once you do it, the next one rolls in and fits right on top, and pretty soon you're in a nice, easy rhythm. It doesn't take a ton of effort. Like spinning a wheel. You give it a tug to get it going, but then it just keeps spinning. Every once in a while, you give it some encouragement. If you want to stop the wheel, you've got to really grab it and counteract that forward motion. It wants to keep spinning. Your progress wants to keep building too. All you have to do is feed it little bits of energy. Let the rhythm carry you forward. Go with it.

### Put the Measuring Stick in the Rear View Mirror

When I started to grow Burnham Law, I had the sole intention of getting better. Everything needed help. Our practice management software, or practice management in general, our hiring, sales, marketing, messaging, communication. . . all of it. And that's even before discussing the practice of law, hiring lawyers who aren't afraid of the courtroom, and all that goes into effective legal representation. And don't forget about the website, marketing, and social media. And if you search for any guides about how to start and grow a reputable law firm, you will only find companies trying to sell you clients, leads, and fear.

I started with focus. Be prepared for court. Brick. Know the case inside and out. Brick. Achieve clients' goals. Brick. I was quality control, chief legal strategist, and marketing director. And I kept stacking those while I started stacking for every other facet of the practice: Supervision brick. Marketing brick. Mentoring brick. Expansion brick. After a while you look up and see what the bricks built, simply by doing the next right thing, taking that next focused step. If something doesn't go right, you don't demolish the brick building. Toss the brick and stack another one. Don't waste precious time eulogizing the brick. It's just one brick. Move on and forward.

## Remarkable Rebounds: Eric Clapton

*"I had good reason to honor his memory and [stay] sober and [try] to do the best that I could to carry a message of that nature to other people."*[63]

The well-known musician, often considered one of the best guitarists of all time, kicked his cocaine habit largely due to his relationship with his young son Conor. In 1991, when he was just four years old, Conor fell out of a 53rd-floor window and died. After the funeral Clapton went home and received the first and only letter his son had ever written him which said, "I love you." Clapton was devastated and hit rock bottom. He moved to Antigua and lived in complete isolation for a year, grieving and playing guitar. Clapton used the pain of that loss to ensure that he remained sober. During this time, he wrote "Tears in Heaven," a song about the loss. It became his best-selling single and a megahit. The loss of his son also led him to develop a deeper connection with his daughter and focus on that relationship.[64]

---

63 Clapton E. (2007, October 11). Eric Clapton On Coming Back From Tragedy. *Access Hollywood.*
64 Clapton E. (2008). *Clapton: The Autobiography.* Broadway Books.

# STEP 6: IMMERSION

*"Constant exposure to these concepts pulls back the curtains to reveal reality–the very clear yet often disguised reality that our lives do not rotate around traumatic events."*

Those who thrive in severe adversity have one final trait in common. They don't dabble in their Comeback. They don't set aside an hour a day to rebuild their future. Instead, they completely immerse themselves in the process. If they aren't stacking bricks, they are sleeping. Period. No backpedaling, no weekends off, no "I'll start tomorrow." They are literally reborn into a new world. Each movie they watch, each podcast, each Google search, each book they read, is a brick–a contributor to the Comeback.

The quickest way to learn Spanish is to move to Spain for a year. Complete immersion in the language. There are no breaks. An English speaker in Spain doesn't get weekends off. They don't stop learning the language when they turn on the TV. They cannot escape from the language. It surrounds them. Those who can't go to Spain will switch their phone, apps, and laptop settings to Spanish only. They only allow themselves to watch Spanish-speaking YouTubers or read books in the Spanish language or watch Spanish movies.

Likewise, we must dive in and surround ourselves with bricks. We are now living in a construction site. We don't leave the site to go home at night. We set up a sleeping bag right there on site and stay there until the building is complete. You can't just read this book and say, "got it," and then go on with your life. You must accept that your old life is gone. Over. You are in Spain now. There is no escape. You now follow different people on social media. You now subscribe to yoga gurus on YouTube and have deleted those true crime channels. You've emptied your fridge of anything that doesn't fuel your mind and body for action. Out of sight, out of mind.

The Six Steps are not something you can fit in during your lunch hour or on Saturday mornings. This. Is. Your. New. Life. It requires a full-on commitment to live the steps in this book. You must embrace being at the bottom if and when you find yourself there again. You must fully embrace your desperation. You must feed your mind and, with added movement, put your inner critic in a timeout and stack your first brick. Immersion is the sixth trait of those who turn trauma into triumph, the CEOs of lemonade. And these leaders have ALL six action steps mastered. Not one or three of five. All Six.

Constant exposure to these concepts pulls back the curtains to reveal reality–the very clear yet often disguised reality that our lives do not rotate around traumatic events. Rather, our lives begin anew every single day. Adversity is just that, adversity. Where you are today is not where you will be tomorrow. You are not your tragedy. You are not walking trauma. You are a person with possibilities and options and strength and power. Immerse yourself in this process, and you will own that power and turn your life around.

CHAPTER 16

# BELIEVE TO BEGIN

Ryan's story showcases how important and effective immersion is. Ryan graduated from the University of Denver College of Law and became a great lawyer. He worked for our firm and was a genuine, authentic, and good human being–one of the best I have ever met. He worked hard and had a wife he adored and three kids who were his world.

At age 42, Ryan became a Colorado State Court Judge. Part of his job was to be on call on weekends for bench warrants when a police officer needs a judge to sign a warrant. Ryan was on call one weekend when one warrant came through. It was for a person in the community, and Ryan knew that his best friend knew this person. Because he had a connection to the case, Ryan recused himself and didn't hear the warrant. However, he did pick up the phone and tell his friend to stay away from this guy for a while. Ryan didn't know that his best friend had been buying cocaine from the guy named in the warrant. He had no idea his friend could be involved in something illegal. All he thought he was doing was suggesting his friend stay away from a dangerous guy for a few days. Ryan ended up being charged with obstructing a federal investigation. He was disbarred and sentenced to serve a year in jail. Ryan had hit bottom.

## Immersion is a Lifestyle

The thing that makes Ryan's story unique is that he had been working at our firm prior to being sentenced. He made a mistake, perhaps several, and in my opinion, he owned it. He resigned from the bench, but he still faced criminal charges.

When Ryan's life fell apart, it really fell apart. He immediately dropped 25 pounds because he couldn't eat. He ended up on an involuntary psych hold because there was a real fear that he was going to take his own life. His entire dream and passion had been practicing law. All that was now gone forever. His family was exposed to humiliation, harassment, and financial harm. He was experiencing very real personal trauma. Ryan was at the absolute worst point in his life. He had hit his rock bottom.

But he had a game plan. Ryan knew that this was his opportunity to be a role model for his children. A light bulb went off for him. He recognized his rock bottom, embraced his desperation, got his mind right, started working out, stacked some bricks while behind bars, and immersed himself in the process. No excuses, no fear, no big goals. Just consistent, forward motion.

## I'm Immersed

The reason I'm here writing this book is because I myself am immersed in the Six Steps. I believe in them so strongly that I can't keep my mouth shut (just ask my wife or my colleagues). Not only do I surround my daily life with movement and meditation and bricks, but I share these tools with others as often as possible. To me, immersing my very existence in forward progression has lifted me out of several rock-bottom situations in my life. And not only have I come back, but I've come back more successfully than before, every single time. I am now at a point where I know and accept that bad things can happen in life, and when the next ones come my way, I am ready to overcome it with these Six Steps. I have a sense of security that, should the worst-case scenario for my life happen tomorrow, it's just a worst-case scenario. I can handle it. Better than that, I can *use* it to become a stronger, more productive person.

In my life in general, I'm an all-or-nothing guy. When I'm in, I'm completely in. And if I'm not completely in, well, then I'm out. I immersed myself in studying law in law school, in learning how to practice law, in beating addiction, in establishing a healthy family, and in building a meaningful, successful law practice. And now I have immersed myself in the Six Steps, my failproof insurance against the next obstacle life will throw at me.

## Remarkable Rebounds: Oprah Winfrey

*"Now, when you're down there in the hole, it looks like failure. When that moment comes, it's okay to feel bad for a little while. Give yourself time to mourn what you think you may have lost. But then, here's the key: Learn from every mistake, because every experience, particularly your mistakes, are there to teach you and force you into being more who you are.*[65]

Oprah Winfrey began life as the child of a single mother in poverty. She was physically abused as a child, then sexually abused as an adolescent. She became pregnant at age 13, and the baby died after birth. This was her rock bottom. Her father helped her find her path forward by emphasizing education, which she credits as turning her life around. She got a scholarship to college and became a broadcast journalist, and eventually became the host of *The Oprah Winfrey Show.* She built a media empire and used her wealth and status to educate girls in Africa at a school she founded. She is one of the most influential personalities of all time with a net worth of $2.6 billion.

---

65 Winfrey O. Harvard Commencement Address. May 30, 2013.

CHAPTER 17

# MORTAR FOR THE BRICKS

*Merriam-Webster* defines immersion as, "Extensive exposure to surroundings or conditions that are native or pertinent to the object of study. Absorbing involvement." For the Six Steps to work, immersion is critical. When we are facing severe adversity and hit rock bottom, we are vulnerable and highly impressionable. It takes only the slightest distraction to derail our climb. In normal life, when you're trying to quit drinking and a friend asks you to come have a beer, you may feel strong enough to say, "Nah, sorry, I'm busy." But when you're at rock bottom and that friend asks you to come have a beer, it is much harder to resist.

Immersion is your stabilizer. It holds your bricks together, defuses all the potential traps, and keeps out the draught. If you've removed that contact from your phone and created a new environment that does not include alcohol in any way, you've eliminated potential traps. Just like cleaning out your fridge when you want to lose 40 pounds, so you don't have to make that choice between a turkey sandwich or a slice of pie. When you are immersed in the Six Steps, there is no way in hell you would even allow a slice of pie to enter your house, because a slice of pie has nothing to do with the construction of your future. If it isn't a part of the construction, it isn't allowed on site.

You can stack all the bricks you want, but something has to stabilize them. The mortar for your bricks is immersion. Immersion cements your bricks together into a solid, robust structure. Without the mortar, you might as well be building a house of cards.

## The Deeper You Go, the Better You Learn

A study published in the journal *Frontiers of Psychology* looked at the impact of immersion on learning a second language.[66] The study found the immersion creates changes in the brain that are not seen with traditional language lessons. When you immerse yourself in a new language, your brain begins to form new networks, responding to a different type of learning that is more significant and long-term than traditional language instruction.

It's not difficult to understand why immersion is critical to your Comeback. You probably know people who have changed their lives by diving completely into a new approach. Shelley, my client with the abusive husband, became immersed in the Six Steps, particularly gaining a powerful interest in Step Four, with Crossfit. It became her passion, her way of life, her guiding principle. It completely changed the focus of her life. This also happens when people join a new religion and go in all the way–that religion changes how they think and respond to every little stimulus in their world. It becomes their guiding principle.

Remember being a kid and suddenly developing a new obsession? Maybe it was a video game or baseball or cheer, or poetry. Whatever it was, you ate, slept, and breathed that new thing. And you became really good at it because it became your entire life. You immersed yourself. In practicing the Six Steps, you have to become that kid again. Surround yourself with anything and everything that contributes to your progression toward that ultimate goal.

By immersing yourself in the Six Steps, they become habits–the same six habits those super survivors have in common. And whether you are in a deep, dark pit right now, or one is waiting around the corner, those six

66 Stein M, Winkler C, Kaiser A, Dierks T. Structural brain changes related to bilingualism: does immersion make a difference? *Front Psychol.* 2014;5:1116.

habits will allow you to take your adversity and use it to build a stronger, better life.

## Immersion Leads to Retention

Other studies have examined how the brains of adults who learned a second language react when they go for a period of time without any practice with the language at all.[67] Those who learned the language through immersion (living in a place or going to a school where only that language was spoken) showed changes in their brain that were similar to those seen in people learning their native language. The immersion learners learned the second language as deeply and as naturally as if it was the language they first learned as children. They retained the language even if they went for a long time without hearing or speaking it. Immersion cemented that language in their brain so deeply that they didn't forget it even when they didn't practice.

When you immerse yourself in something completely, it becomes as natural to you as the first language you learned. If you dive in and live the Six Steps, they will become a part of you. Your brain will change to incorporate the steps into the way you approach the world. These six habits will stick with you throughout your life and pop right back into your brain anytime you face severe adversity or trauma.

## Immersion Through Visualization

Olympic athletes regularly use a technique called visualization to help their performance.[68] They mentally visualize themselves doing every single

---

67 Georgetown University Medical Center. "In immersion foreign language learning, adults attain, retain native speaker brain pattern." *ScienceDaily.* 28 March 2012.

68 Ridderinkhof KR, Brass M. How Kinesthetic Motor Imagery works: A predictive-processing theory of visualization

movement needed to complete their challenge. For example, divers mentally see themselves standing on the diving platform and then move their mind through every single movement they need to take before hitting the water. Skiers visualize themselves going down the mountain, taking every turn and every jump, controlling their skis, poles, and bodies.

By immersing themselves in a mental video of what they need to do, these athletes are able to prepare their minds and bodies to achieve their goals, even when they aren't out on the field. There are several studies that show exactly why this works. In one study, basketball players who regularly visualized themselves making free throws improved their free-throw skill by 23 percent. Long jumpers who visualized their jumps improved by 43 percent. Visualization trains our brains just as effectively as physical action itself.

Athletes who use this technique generally visualize every single detail of the event. They see the surroundings, smell the air, hear the sounds, feel the air temperature, and feel wherever their body or feet are positioned. Then they mentally see every single movement they need to make. They completely immerse their entire selves in the experience of their sport, without actually being there. So, while a gold medal gymnast isn't in the gym 24/7, they are still able to immerse themselves in progressing toward their ultimate goal–even as they lie in bed preparing to sleep. And doing so gives them a tremendous advantage. More evidence of the extreme power of immersion. My 10-year-old daughter, Clara will regularly ask Katy and I what she should dream about. Without knowing it, she is opening herself up to her intentions.

---

in sports and motor expertise. *Journal of Physiology-Paris.* Volume 109, Issues 1–3. 2015. 53-63.

## Immersion and Careers

Immersion also helps people develop musical talent and skills. Like the gymnast, the concert pianist can immerse herself in practicing her craft even when she is in the shower (where the grand piano doesn't fit). By playing a recording of her music piece over and over, she trains her brain to recognize every note, every series of notes, the pattern and flow. By the time she gets back on the piano bench, her fingers seem to move by themselves. The brain knows what to do, because the musician has immersed herself in their music even while she is away from the piano.

Immersion is used in many career training pathways. Professional programs like medical school and law school are notorious for doling out so much work that the student has time for nothing but study and sleep. On average, 80 to 90 hours a week of study and work are required to graduate. Through this level of immersion, these students are capable of learning extreme amounts of information with impressive recall. Later in their careers, any number of situations could arise, and they would know how to handle it, fast, with no warning and no preparation.

Military boot camp is another form of immersion, where new recruits must follow a grueling program for weeks to mold them into soldiers. Through immersion, soldiers are able to respond to sudden and violent attacks with clarity and action. They have *become* soldiers. They don't turn it off and on. There is no off.

Immersing yourself allows you to program your brain to function at high capacity through uncomfortable and unpredictable situations. This is how Olympic medalists are able to perform under extreme pressure, how musicians are able to play perfectly with butterflies in their stomach and thousands of people watching. The point of immersion is to develop an 'autopilot,' a mode you will automatically enter into that allows you to perform at maximum capacity even in emergency situations. By immersing yourself in the Six Steps, the six traits become so ingrained that you will respond automatically when trouble arises.

## How to Achieve Immersion

Like the guy who moves to Spain or puts his phone on Spanish-mode to learn Spanish, if you are going to immerse yourself in the Six Steps, you've got to remove anything that doesn't contribute to the life you are constructing. If you aren't sure whether something belongs on your construction site, ask yourself whether it contributes even in the slightest bit to rebuilding your life. If you cannot see a contribution, you don't need it.

There are likely some apps on your phone that could be deleted. Video games are awesome, but I have yet to come up with a single way they contribute to progression. "But Candy Crush helps me relax!" So does a bottle of wine or watching a funny movie. None of these are productive in any way. Are you then to assume that you will never be able to relax again? You'll never be able to have fun? That's your inner critic again, throwing a fit because they can't do what they want. Of course, you can relax and have fun. Does ziplining sound fun? Does swimming sound fun? Or dancing? Does sitting in a jacuzzi listening to a podcast on cooking or mountaineering or traveling sound relaxing? Or maybe getting a pillow and blanket and watching a movie about someone who surmounted some insane obstacle?

The point of immersion is to make smart decisions. Every action you take should be a forward-moving action. Even if you want to lay in bed all day, that's fine. But browse social media or watch movies that inspire and teach. A comedy may make you laugh temporarily, but the key word there is temporarily. Just think about it. Weigh your bricks. Should you watch Predator or Rocky? Should you do a five-minute shower or watch five minutes of TikTok? If you want to watch TikTok, do it while walking. Save it for the treadmill.

Personalize your immersion so that it works for you. You know what your triggers are, your weaknesses and strengths. Get rid of any potential traps and immerse yourself in a forward-moving, fun, relaxing, productive, creative, motivating, inspirational environment.

## Change Your Story

We are the narrators of our own stories· As we go through life, we're summarizing things and making conclusions about ourselves and our loved ones. When you are at your rock bottom, the story you are telling yourself is likely not a good one. Remember how I sat in the MRI waiting room telling myself my life was basically over?

To adopt the Six Steps, they have to become the story you are telling yourself. If you are at rock bottom and you tell yourself it's over, I'll never recover, that's a story that you're telling yourself (and believing!). But if you hit rock bottom and say OK, I see, this is rock bottom, but I am desperate, I have a positive mindset, I move my body, and I am going to stack bricks to come back better than ever, that is a different story that you tell yourself and that you come to believe. You control the narration of your life story. No one else is narrating! (And if someone in your life is trying to narrate for you, they aren't the kind of person you want in your life.) Make the Six Steps your story, and you will find yourself coming back from trauma, or preferably smaller problems, better and bigger than ever.

Research has shown that self-talk is important in changing your perception of yourself.[69] There is one tiny tweak you can make to the self-talk you're already doing that is going to drastically increase its impact. Instead of talking to yourself and saying things like, "I am stacking bricks and creating success," get rid of 'I.' Instead, say, "Jasmine, you are stacking bricks and creating success." Using your name instead of the pronoun 'I' tricks your mind into thinking someone else is saying these things to you. This carries more authority than inner dialogue.

Have you ever done something stupid like run a red light or dropped an egg on the floor and said to yourself, "Nice move, Maria"? We tend to use the third person when we talk to ourselves about mistakes, but if we can get into the habit of using it when we talk to ourselves about our plans, our futures, our identities, and our successes, that self-talk will have a much heftier impact on us. Granted, it can be a little obnoxious when you hear other people talking about themselves in the third person (some athletes do this in interviews and have been teased about it). But you don't have to talk out loud, just change your thoughts to use your formal name.

When you are immersed in a new world, career, or language, and you live only that, you quickly establish proficiency. Immerse yourself in the Six Steps and let them become your language. Use them to weigh your next steps, use them as your guide. Change your story into one about someone who overcomes all obstacles. Get into the flow, the motion, the forward dynamic, and let it carry you.

---

69 Cascio CN, O'Donnell MB, Tinney FJ, et al. Self-affirmation activates brain systems associated with self-related processing and reward and is reinforced by future orientation. *Soc Cogn Affect Neurosci.* 2016;11(4):621-629.

## Remarkable Rebounds: Kobe Bryant

*"You have to be open-minded and not be rigid. If you're rigid, that's weakness. All you can do is forget about the bad stuff and then move on. You just kind of roll with it, you just kind of learn. I will not make the same mistakes in the future that I have made in the past. I will make new mistakes, I am sure. And I will learn from them, too. You have to be fluid. Your body changes. As that happens, your moves need to change, your training program needs to change, you have to be able to adapt."*[70]

Kobe Bryant was a Philadelphia-born, Italy-raised, son of a former NBA player. At age 18, after his first big break, playing basketball for the Lakers, the rookie Bryant shot four air balls, losing the must-win playoff game to the Utah Jazz. And this was only the beginning. Bryant faced incredible obstacles during his 20-year career. He struggled with severe knee and ankle injuries, was accused of rape in 2003, and endured constant media scrutiny for his controversial claims about fellow NBA players and referees. But amid injuries, controversy, and criticism, Bryant pushed through to become one of the greatest NBA players of all time, winning five NBA championships and two Olympic gold medals, making 18 consecutive All-Star game appearances and two NBA Final MVPs, becoming a two-time NBA scoring champion, and shooting an 81-point game with a 60-point career finale.

---

70 Sager, M. (2007, November). Kobe Bryant Doesn't Want Your Love. *Esquire.*

CHAPTER 18

# GET IN, THE WATER'S WARM

I talked to Ryan two days before he was going to go to jail. He said, "What kind of diet do you think they are going to allow me to have in the commissary?" I scratched my head at this one. This guy's life has imploded, and he's thinking about the prison food? I asked him what he was getting at, and he said he was going to come out of his sentence healthy and focused, get into the best shape of his life both mentally and physically–so that when he was released, he'd be at peak status to enjoy life and move forward.

## Case Study: Malik

Malik was able to change his life because he lived and breathed the Six Steps. They became a part of him. When I met Malik, he was at rock bottom, not ready to admit he was at the lowest possible point. His life was shattered. And he didn't want to be reminded of it in any way. He wanted to escape into distraction and denial. If he had carried on like this, he would have likely ended up with more DUIs, more arrests, or worse. It is unlikely he could have kept his dad out of a nursing home under those circumstances. He wouldn't have seen a path forward. And he definitely would not have believed that he could take the incredibly low point in his life and rebuild things to an even better situation.

I go have dinner at his restaurant when I'm in town. It always thrills me to see Malik come out in his white chef's coat. He's incredibly talented. Since his jail sentence, he's faced other types of adversity: his beloved girlfriend of three years cheated on him, he was diagnosed with an irregular heartbeat and had to get a pacemaker implant, and the pandemic pushed hard against his business. But because Malik had immersed himself in making the Six Steps a part of him, ingrained them into his very way of life, he went into autopilot every time something terrible happened. He felt pain and fear and anxiety, but all the while his mind was working its magic, allowing him to accept he'd hit rock bottom once again, embrace his desperation, and get his mind right. His physical activity didn't waver. He focused on laying that next brick, and he stayed immersed in a forward thinking, creative, inspirational, motivating environment.

Malik didn't have to put forth some crazy level of additional effort during the rough times because the path was already there. He was able to see opportunity and creative solutions. During the pandemic, he started selling sourdough starters and a super creative takeout menu. Feeling pain, fear, or anxiety happened, but it did not derail him. Like a soldier, musician, gymnast, or ER doctor, when the pressure hit hard, he went into autopilot. Immersion gave him total recall and clarity when adrenaline was high. Not only has Malik come back from his worst-case scenario, but he continually uses adversity to renovate his life (and he's got the best risotto in town).

## Immersion Pays Off

As for Ryan, while he was waiting to be sentenced, he went to every single one of his kids' sporting and school events. Time with his family was adding bricks to his renovation. Once he learned he was going to jail, he stacked another brick by figuring out what he could eat in prison so he could develop a workout regimen. He learned he would have access to books in jail and could spend a good chunk of time studying and preparing for a new career. Desperate people do desperate, creative, incredible things.

Ryan wasn't trying to distract himself by drinking himself into blackout every night. He wasn't worrying how he was going to support himself when he got out of prison or how he was going to hang on to his innocent and trusting family. And he was not looking at giant goals he might never achieve. Ryan knew the drill.

It's one thing to say, "I'm going to get my mind right," but when you're on trial and the Judge is about to sentence you to one to three years in jail, and all you can think about is how you are going to use that time to create something magnificent, to me that's the definition of living. Accepting your bad decision, accepting your bad luck, and knowing that tomorrow is a new day with new bricks to stack.

## Practice Makes Progress

Ryan's example shows the importance of immersing yourself in these Six Steps. Because he had already taught himself the Six Steps and ingrained them in his daily life, severe adversity didn't destroy him. I'm not talking about laughing when the sky falls on you. Trauma is traumatic, that's part of the process. You aren't at rock bottom if you haven't fallen apart. And there are many ways to fall apart. The Six Steps do not mean you won't feel trauma, won't be devastated, or won't be in a full crisis. Of course, you will fall apart when the worst happens. That's what trauma does to us. What the Six Steps does is give you a way out, a way up, a clear path to tackle any situation, and to come back better.

When you live the Six Steps, it becomes your mindset. Even if you are carefully stacking your bricks and you've got some momentum and a tornado comes and blows those bricks down, you'll be able to keep stacking them because you know how to do it and it has become second nature for you. Stacking bricks will not only get you out of the trauma, but it will help you change anything else in your life that you want to work on: your job, your family, your relationships, your health, your hobbies, your skills, your attitude. If you adopt the practice, it will move you forward in all aspects of your life.

## Visualization as Immersion

The technique that athletes use to see their success works for trauma too. You can apply the same technique to immerse yourself in the Six Steps. Take the time to visualize your situation. Feel the trauma. Really let yourself accept it and be in it. Sink into the desperation. And visualize yourself with a resilient, positive mindset. Imagine what it will feel like. Picture yourself doing yoga in the morning, what the room looks like, what each muscle feels as it stretches. Anytime you can't be actively moving forward, do it mentally. Visualize it.

Remember to add in as much detail as you can when you visualize each step. Let yourself feel the trauma and despair. See how the world will look to you when you approach it with a positive mindset. Imagine how your legs and arms and back and abs will feel when you incorporate physical movement into your life. Walk yourself through your next brick. See what you have to say, do, get, or change to stack that one brick. If you are going to add a meditation practice to your life, use part of your meditation time for visualization. The more you see yourself following the Six Steps, the more acclimated your brain will be to them. Soon they will just become second nature, just as they did for Ryan.

## Immersion Changes Your Response

When you immerse yourself in these steps and turn to them every time you face serious adversity, they become part of your immediate reaction to challenges. When you see, live, and breathe the Six Steps, your brain will automatically start to apply them. After you've adapted to these steps, you won't have to think about them anymore. Your entire approach to adversity will change, and your brain will automatically know that when things go badly, the way to handle them is through these Six Steps.

These six traits not only change how you think and behave; they change how other people see you. When I think about Ryan, I don't see a guy who got in trouble. I see a resilient, intelligent, creative role model. Deploying the Six Steps will change how you react to the world around you, and others are going to see it and use your example in their own adversity.

This has been the result of me changing the way I practice law. I immersed myself in the Six Steps and as a result I turned our law practice into one that is completely real and straightforward, cluing people into exactly what their options are and what they are facing. Clients appreciated our transparency. My family noticed. My friends noticed. Once I'd identified the six traits of people who thrive after trauma and started experimenting with them in my own life, I saw change not only in myself and my circumstances, but in the people around me, in how they perceived me, and in my approach to life.

## Create a New Identity

A part of immersion is changing the world around you. That inevitably requires you to change the identity you create for yourself. You are born into a new environment as a brand-new person. This ties into the story that you're telling yourself. If you tell yourself that life is over, that you have no chance of rebuilding your life, that is then who you are. But you aren't that. You are a new person. The old person has been replaced through knowledge, strength, and power.

If you tell yourself the story that you are going to come back better than ever, that you are a person who rebounds, that you are the type that scales Mount Everest for breakfast, that becomes your identity. You're a champion boxer. Bring on the punches. And when your inner critic sneaks in and says, "Stop being ridiculous," you tell that poor little impatient thing to take a back seat and chill. Because you are going into the ring, like it or not. Noticing all of these things reaffirms for your brain that you ARE a powerful force who can handle whatever is thrown your way. Get into the pool. Not just a toe, all the way in. Immerse yourself in the steps. Make them your way of life. Swim in them. Let them hold you up. The water's warm. You're going to love it, I promise.

## Remarkable Rebounds: Larry King

*"You can't have happiness without having had unhappiness, because how else would you know what's happy?"*[71]

Late-night talk show host Larry King was not very well-known in the 70s, but he was beginning to make a name for himself. Some bad business decisions plus multiple divorces led to him having to file for bankruptcy. He was also charged with grand larceny for stealing from a business partner (those charges were later dropped). This was his rock bottom. That same year he was offered a national radio talk show which eventually became a TV show that ran for 25 years. He won many, many broadcasting awards including an Emmy. When he died, his estate was valued at $144 million.

71 Fussman C. Larry King: What I've Learned. *Esquire.* August 9, 2010.

# CONCLUSION

The ability to come back from trauma and adversity stronger than before is so interesting to me. If we can come back better from anything that's out there, then why isn't everyone doing it? As I see it, there are two reasons. First, we aren't talking about it. Look up trauma online and you'll get an eyeful of how damaging and debilitating it is (and it is). But no one seems to point out that damaging and debilitating are necessary and perfectly normal parts of life. Human beings are sculptures, molded and pressed and chipped away at until we become the final masterpiece. Damage comes with the territory. We get one life, and without trauma and pain and fear and all the other ingredients that make us who we are, the great role models we look up to would never have become role models at all.

Second, people don't talk about rebounding from trauma because we haven't clearly defined the differences between those who give up and those who thrive. Why some people come back from trauma and others just don't. And in many cases, when the ingredients of life renovation ARE defined, they mention things like manifesting wealth, making vision boards, repeating positive affirmations, which in my opinion are generally not helpful at all without specific action.

What I've learned from the thousands of people I interacted with who have gone through adversity or trauma is that some give up and some thrive and succeed. Those who thrive have six traits in common, six habits, the Six Steps in this book. Those who do all six, not one or three or five, but all six, are the ones who turn adversity into gold.

Life is a series of ups and downs; there is no avoiding it. As a lawyer, I believe I have a responsibility not only to pull my clients out of their legal crisis, but to send them on their way with valuable tools for their Comeback–for building a new and better life. Anything else is just a band-aid, and not a true solution. I would never recommend something that I didn't personally try. The Six Steps continue to inspire me over and over again, every time I face a major challenge in my life. Burnham Law grew once I attacked challenges with the right mindset. Burnham Law got better as I got better as a leader, and that was only possible by experiencing adversity after failure after trauma. And repeat. A failure is a gift, an exposed weakness solidified. So, solidify it, and move on.

Our clients are getting quality legal help. They are also getting a road map on how to build their lives to an even higher level than where they started, something we desperately need when we've faced a divorce, custody case, bankruptcy, DUI, jail time, business closure, a loved one's death, or some other personal or business trauma. Not only have our clients taken our advice to heart and built healthy, fruitful lives, they are also able to advise their friends and family on how to move forward from trauma.

I fully understand how hard it is to be at a rock-bottom moment. There's no hope. You've lost something you can never get back. Your life will never be the same. I also understand that it's a part of being human. And while we will always have memories of our lives before trauma, we are going to make new ones. We are about to experience even bigger and better things. It is healthy and important to mourn the loss of the past. Don't deny yourself that. And while you are grieving, listen to the desperation. It is pulling you to do great things. And you will.

Mahalo!

## ABOUT THE AUTHOR

Todd Burnham, founding partner and mindset coach at Burnham Law, is an author, keynote speaker, adjunct professor (@ CU Law), mentor, entrepreneur, former All-American lacrosse player, and host of the podcast, Deep Bench with Todd Burnham. With his passion for business, his no-BS leadership approach, and sheer determination, Todd took his law firm from an unfinished basement to an elite seven-office, multi-state law firm. Now, in *COMEBACK: Epic Rebound Strategies for Personal or Business Adversity,* Todd compiles his warrior mentality, aggressive insight, and competitive resolve into a set of revolutionary maneuvers that have helped countless individuals turn severe adversity into unprecedented triumph. Todd's unique motivation style and raw sense of humor are a welcome change from the motivational and business advice you're used to hearing. Whether you're a burgeoning entrepreneur or a seasoned professional, COMEBACK is sure to inspire you to get your mind right, take action, and soar. Todd currently consults with law firms on mindset, marketing, and growth strategies. He divides his time between Boulder, Colorado and Kauai, Hawaii.

# APPENDIX

## Mental Health Resources

The Six Steps in this book are the key to fueling your Comeback. However, certain underlying mental health issues must first be addressed to successfully implement the program, including:

- Suicidal ideation
- Substance abuse disorder
- Persistent depressive disorder
- Generalized anxiety disorder (GAD)
- Panic disorder
- Post-traumatic stress disorder (PTSD)
- Obsessive-compulsive disorder (OCD)
- Social or material phobias
- Bipolar disorder
- Schizophrenia

In 2020, an estimated 21 percent of adults in the U.S. (52.9 million) were diagnosed with a mental illness.[72] Seeking out a counselor or doctor can be your golden ticket to a successful and productive future.

Numerous forms of highly effective therapeutic and treatment approaches are widely accessible.

72 2020 National Survey on Drug Use and Health (NSDUH). Substance Abuse and Mental Health Services Administration (SAMHSA).

Most resources listed below are **available 24/7 and offer online chat, email, text messaging, or phone calls:**

**Suicidal Ideation**

- Dial 911 – in case of life-threatening emergency
- 1-800-273-TALK (8255) – 24-hour National Suicide Prevention Lifeline
- Online chat with a counselor – https://suicidepreventionlifeline.org/chat/
- For the hearing impaired – TTY at: 1-800-799-4889
- Dial 988 – U.S. Mental Health Crisis Hotline

**Substance Abuse Disorder**

- Dial 911 – in case of life-threatening emergency/overdose
- 1-800-273-TALK (8255) – 24-hour National Suicide Prevention Lifeline
- Online chat with a counselor – https://suicidepreventionlifeline.org/chat/
- 1-800-662-4357 – Substance Abuse and Mental Health Services Administration (SAMHSA)
- www.FindTreatment.gov – to locate treatment provider in your area
- 1-866-972-0134 – AA hotline – sobriety support, locate AA meetings in your area, find rehab facilities or detox options

**Depressive Disorder**

- Dial 911 – in case of life-threatening emergency
- 1-800-273-TALK (8255) – 24-hour National Suicide Prevention Lifeline
- Online chat with a counselor – https://suicidepreventionlifeline.org/chat/

- 1-866-903-3787 – 24-hour National Mental Health Hotline
- 1-877-870-4673 – Samaritans emotional support hotline
- Text "HOME" to 741741 – Crisis Text Line
- 1- 800-971-0016 – Friendship Line / Wellness Checks
- 1-800-273-8255 (press 1) – Veterans Crisis Line
- Text 838255 – Veterans Crisis Line
- 1-800-273-8255 – Crisis Support Line
- Text "CARE" to 839863 – Crisis Support Line
- 1-800-950-6264 – National Alliance on Mental Illness (NAMI) Helpline
- Email info@nami.org – National Alliance on Mental Illness (NAMI) Helpline

**Generalized Anxiety Disorder (GAD)**

- Dial 911 – in case of life-threatening emergency
- 1-800-273-TALK (8255) – 24-hour National Suicide Prevention Lifeline
- Online chat with a counselor – https://suicidepreventionlifeline.org/chat/
- 1-866-903-3787 – 24-hour National Mental Health Hotline
- 1-877-870-4673 – Samaritans emotional support hotline
- Text "HOME" to 741741 – Crisis Text Line
- 1- 800-971-0016 – Friendship Line / Wellness Checks
- 1-800-273-8255 (press 1) – Veterans Crisis Line
- Text 838255 – Veterans Crisis Line
- 1-800-273-8255 – Crisis Support Line
- Text "CARE" to 839863 – Crisis Support Line
- 1-800-950-6264 – National Alliance on Mental Illness (NAMI) Helpline

- Email info@nami.org – National Alliance on Mental Illness (NAMI) Helpline

**Panic Disorder**

- Dial 911 – in case of life-threatening emergency
- 1-800-273-TALK (8255) – 24-hour National Suicide Prevention Lifeline
- Online chat with a counselor – https://suicidepreventionlifeline.org/chat/
- 1-866-903-3787 – 24-hour National Mental Health Hotline
- 1-877-870-4673 – Samaritans emotional support hotline
- Text "HOME" to 741741 – Crisis Text Line
- 1- 800-971-0016 – Friendship Line / Wellness Checks
- 1-800-273-8255 (press 1) – Veterans Crisis Line
- Text 838255 – Veterans Crisis Line
- 1-800-273-8255 – Crisis Support Line
- Text "CARE" to 839863 – Crisis Support Line
- 1-800-950-6264 – National Alliance on Mental Illness (NAMI) Helpline
- Email info@nami.org – National Alliance on Mental Illness (NAMI) Helpline

**Post-Traumatic Stress Disorder (PTSD)**

- Dial 911 – in case of life-threatening emergency
- 1-800-273-TALK (8255) – 24-hour National Suicide Prevention Lifeline
- Online chat with a counselor – https://suicidepreventionlifeline.org/chat/
- 1-866-903-3787 – 24-hour National Mental Health Hotline

- 1-877-870-4673 – Samaritans emotional support hotline
- Text "HOME" to 741741 – Crisis Text Line
- 1- 800-971-0016 – Friendship Line / Wellness Checks
- 1-800-273-8255 (press 1) – Veterans Crisis Line
- Text 838255 – Veterans Crisis Line
- 1-800-273-8255 – Crisis Support Line
- Text "CARE" to 839863 – Crisis Support Line
- 1-800-950-6264 – National Alliance on Mental Illness (NAMI) Helpline
- Email info@nami.org – National Alliance on Mental Illness (NAMI) Helpline

**Obsessive-Compulsive Disorder (OCD)**

- Dial 911 – in case of life-threatening emergency
- 1-800-273-TALK (8255) – 24-hour National Suicide Prevention Lifeline
- Online chat with a counselor – https://suicidepreventionlifeline.org/chat/
- 1-866-903-3787 – 24-hour National Mental Health Hotline
- 1-877-870-4673 – Samaritans emotional support hotline
- Text "HOME" to 741741 – Crisis Text Line
- 1- 800-971-0016 – Friendship Line / Wellness Checks
- 1-800-273-8255 (press 1) – Veterans Crisis Line
- Text 838255 – Veterans Crisis Line
- 1-800-273-8255 – Crisis Support Line
- Text "CARE" to 839863 – Crisis Support Line
- 1-800-950-6264 – National Alliance on Mental Illness (NAMI) Helpline

- Email info@nami.org – National Alliance on Mental Illness (NAMI) Helpline

**Social or Material Phobias**

- Dial 911 – in case of life-threatening emergency
- 1-800-273-TALK (8255) – 24-hour National Suicide Prevention Lifeline
- Online chat with a counselor – https://suicidepreventionlifeline.org/chat/
- 1-866-903-3787 – 24-hour National Mental Health Hotline
- 1-877-870-4673 – Samaritans emotional support hotline
- Text "HOME" to 741741 – Crisis Text Line
- 1- 800-971-0016 – Friendship Line / Wellness Checks
- 1-800-273-8255 (press 1) – Veterans Crisis Line
- Text 838255 – Veterans Crisis Line
- 1-800-273-8255 – Crisis Support Line
- Text "CARE" to 839863 – Crisis Support Line
- 1-800-950-6264 – National Alliance on Mental Illness (NAMI) Helpline
- Email info@nami.org – National Alliance on Mental Illness (NAMI) Helpline

**Bipolar Disorder**

- Dial 911 – in case of life-threatening emergency
- 1-800-273-TALK (8255) – 24-hour National Suicide Prevention Lifeline
- Online chat with a counselor – https://suicidepreventionlifeline.org/chat/

- 1-866-903-3787 – 24-hour National Mental Health Hotline
- 1-877-870-4673 – Samaritans emotional support hotline
- Text "HOME" to 741741 – Crisis Text Line
- 1- 800-971-0016 – Friendship Line / Wellness Checks
- 1-800-273-8255 (press 1) – Veterans Crisis Line
- Text 838255 – Veterans Crisis Line
- 1-800-273-8255 – Crisis Support Line
- Text "CARE" to 839863 – Crisis Support Line
- 1-800-950-6264 – National Alliance on Mental Illness (NAMI) Helpline
- Email info@nami.org – National Alliance on Mental Illness (NAMI) Helpline
- Bipolar Disorder Support Group: https://www.bphope.com/community/
- Bipolar Disorder Group Meetings: https://www.dbsalliance.org/

**Schizophrenia**

- Dial 911 – in case of life-threatening emergency
- 1-800-273-TALK (8255) – 24-hour National Suicide Prevention Lifeline
- Online chat with a counselor – https://suicidepreventionlifeline.org/chat/
- 1-866-903-3787 – 24-hour National Mental Health Hotline
- 1-877-870-4673 – Samaritans emotional support hotline
- Text "HOME" to 741741 – Crisis Text Line
- 1- 800-971-0016 – Friendship Line / Wellness Checks
- 1-800-273-8255 (press 1) – Veterans Crisis Line
- Text 838255 – Veterans Crisis Line

- 1-800-273-8255 – Crisis Support Line
- Text "CARE" to 839863 – Crisis Support Line
- 1-800-950-6264 – National Alliance on Mental Illness (NAMI) Helpline
- Email info@nami.org – National Alliance on Mental Illness (NAMI) Helpline

## Suggested Reading

The following books have had a positive impact on my life in one way or another and deserve mention. In addition, I suggest you research your own books of interest. No time to read? Try audiobooks–a blessing for the multitasker.

Bach, Richard. (2006). *The Bridge Across Forever.*

Chouinard, Yvon. (2016). *Let My People Go Surfing.*

Dyer, Wayne. (2002). *Getting In the Gap.*

Hall, Kevin. (2010). *Aspire: Discovering Your Purpose Through the Power of Words*

Harris, Dan. (2014). *10% Happier: How I Tamed the Voice in My Head, Reduced Stress Without Losing My Edge, and Found Self-Help That Actually Works — A True Story.*

Hill, Napoleon. (1937). *Think and Grow Rich.*

Hollis, James. (2006). *Finding Meaning in the Second Half of Life.*

Kiyosaki, Robert T. (2011). *Rich Dad, Poor Dad.*

McConaughey, Matthew. (2020). *Greenlights.*

Millman, Dan. (2006). *Way of the Peaceful Warrior: A Book That Changes Lives.*

Rey, Neila. (2016). *100 No-Equipment Workouts.* Vol. 1-4.

Ruiz, Don Miguel. (2018). *The Four Agreements: A Practical Guide to Personal Freedom.*

Singer, Michael A. (2007). *The Unthethered Soul.*

Tolle, Eckhart. (2004). *The Power of Now.*

## Quick Six-Steps Reference Chart

You can begin implementing all Six Steps today, right now, and get your Comeback ball rolling. Are you practicing each step daily? Bookmark this reference chart summing up the Six Steps. Use it as a checklist to help you stay on track, flip to it anytime you need a boost!

### Step 1: Hit Bottom

Ask yourself where you're at in your life right at this minute. Have things been better? Worse? Acknowledge your place. Don't try to distract yourself or deny your circumstances. Recognize your situation for what it is. This recognition holds great power.

Allow yourself to experience despair, panic, sorrow, fear, anger. These feelings are as much a part of life as joy and elation and peace. Do not compare your situation to the hardships of others or past experiences of your own. Rock bottom is relative. Remember that your own rock bottom is your individual low at that time, in that situation, and in that area of your life. Own it. Use it.

## Step 2: Embrace Desperation

Are you feeling desperate? Are you appreciating the feeling? Desperation in response to severe trauma and adversity is a healthy survival tool. If you wish to rebuild your life using the adverse and troubling events you experience, you must embrace that feeling of desperation, understand that it drives the human urge to fight for ourselves, our families, and our society.

In a state of desperation, our minds provide us with sight. We are able to detect opportunities we are typically blind to. We are able to derive and implement incredibly creative solutions that, without desperation, would seem impossible. Trauma and adversity push us toward change using the fuel of desperation. Rather than fearing or denying your desperate state, embrace it. Allow the energy of your desperation to rocket you up and out of your rock bottom.

## Step 3: Get Your Mind Right

Are you exploring and becoming familiar with your own mind and spirit? Try techniques that feed your confidence, security, and cognitive clarity–all important resources when coming back from trauma. Meditation, spirituality, gratitude, mindfulness, and other similar practices are life changers. These tools are not a one-size-fits-all. Try a handful off approaches. Experiment. Which ones do you enjoy? Which ones do you feel are making an impact? Gratitude practices? Meditation? Choose one or several and continue to learn. Don't aim for perfection. Just read and practice. We are (and always will be) a work in progress.

Don't fall for "positive thinking" approaches that promote procrastination, distraction, or denial. For example, don't try to 'manifest' your future, cite positive affirmations over and over, or make a vision board of all the things you want. These behaviors waste valuable time and energy with zero measurable payoff. Instead, become familiar with your own mind through the effective and proven tools mentioned in Step 3. Finding a practice that supports and enhances your mental state is essential in keeping your inner critic at bay and creating a mental paradigm shift. You cannot build a better life until you get your mind right.

## Step 4: Move

Are you moving your body at least 90 minutes per week? Step 4 is not about losing weight or becoming physically fit. Step 4 is about saturating your brain with the oxygen and nutrients it needs to think clearly and creatively, to detect opportunities and make decisions in the midst of high-stress situations. Physical movement–muscle contraction, stretching, increasing the heart rate, and breathing–are vital to proper brain function.

Just 90 minutes a week of physical activity improves mental clarity, creativity, memory, decision making, and cognitive ability. When the brain is functioning under an optimal environment, it produces feelings of strength, optimism, and motivation–essential components for a powerful rebound.

## Step 5: Stack Bricks

Are you focused on the next step forward? Or envisioning the big goals you have for yourself? Don't fall into the trap of wasting time and energy inspecting the forest. Instead, inspect each individual tree. Aim big, miss big. Aim small, miss small. Take one, small, achievable action before even thinking of the next. Rebuild your life brick by brick.

No one builds a skyscraper by chunking the completed project down.

Rather, they focus on installing one bolt, then the next, until one day they look up and the project is complete. You should be doing the same. Focus only on the very next step you can take to rebuild your life, whether it be brushing your teeth or revising your resume. Then reward yourself for each small win. Better yet, reward yourself *during the process* of each small step. Your small wins will snowball into big change.

## Step 6: Immersion

Are you practicing the Six Steps one hour a day? Each night after work? Are you surrounding yourself with these habits every waking moment? Immersion is key to integrating your tools into your life and accessing them even in the toughest of times. Like an Olympic athlete or a military soldier, like a person who moved to Spain to learn the Spanish language, immersion in your new life practices will take you leaps and bounds farther than brief, intermittent application.

Through immersion, you gain a road map to guide you through any adverse event in your life. Delete those time-wasting phone apps. Tell your drinking buddies you're busy tonight. Make new friendships with people who support your interests–online or in real life. Watch inspiring movies when you settle in at night. Listen to inspiring podcasts while you drive to work. Immerse your entire surroundings in the rebuilding process–in fun, enjoyable, and relaxing ways. Immersion is key.

## Share The Wealth

Interested in helping guide a loved one, employee, or coworker through trauma or adversity? Here are some important Do's and Don'ts:

**Do**

Watch for red flags. Times of trauma and adversity are dark. It is not uncommon for people to react in unhealthy ways, with self-harm, substance abuse, or isolation. Stay aware of any changes in your friend's appearance or behavior. If you suspect an unhealthy situation, encourage your friend to seek professional help. If your friend broke their leg, you would help them to call a doctor. If your friend is struggling mentally, do the same, help them call a mental health professional.

**Don't**

Feel you are intruding. It is easy for us to want to let a friend's depression ride itself out, not to pry or ask too many questions. Some may think they would just make things worse by bringing up the adverse situation. However, being supportive and encouraging includes taking the time to show you care. When you are alone with your friend, ask how they are doing. Ask them if they need help with anything. Offer to do an activity with them. Don't pressure them, but make them feel comfortable to open up to you when they are ready.

**Do**

Help steer the mindset away from fear and toward change. Example: A friend has lost their license to practice medicine, and you notice they are drinking heavily and appear disheveled and tired. Direct conversation toward opportunities and the advantages of a career change. Suggest adventures like travel and new activities to redirect perspective.

**Don't**

Feed negative conversations. Example: A friend has been fired from their management position and comes to you complaining about their asshole boss. Don't reply with, "Yeah, she's some piece of work!" Instead, reply with, "You were WAY too talented for that job. Can't wait to see what you do next!"

**Do**

Share links to videos, books, and websites suggesting fun physical activities. Invite your friend to go hiking, ziplining, bowling, skating, rock climbing, surfing, swimming, geocaching, biking, go-cart riding, anything active. Share short (5-10 minute) yoga or at-home workout videos. Challenge them to move for fun.

**Don't**

Promote behaviors that do not align with progression and change. Examples: Going out to a bar for drinks, binging Netflix shows with little positive value, sharing apps for phone games. Avoid promoting behaviors that are distracting. Distraction, while temporarily relieving, does much more damage than good, wasting valuable time and energy.

**Do**

Practice patience. Do not allow yourself to become affected when your friend becomes irritable, depressed, or anxious. These behaviors are normal and natural responses to severe adversity and trauma. If your friend is crying, let them cry and be there to support them. If your friend snaps at you for not being supportive or not understanding their situation, don't snap back. Instead, agree with them, listen to their feelings. Listening is much more powerful than talking. If you don't know what to say, don't talk. Just listen.

**Don't**

Compare the situation to other hard situations. Each individual's hardships are difficult. Appreciate that difficulty and pain. Don't try to minimize the problem by comparing it to other hard times in their lives or the lives of others. Show that you understand how difficult their situation is and recognize their feelings in each moment. No two people experience pain, fear, or anxiety in the same way. Learn from your friend how they are feeling, and understand that their feelings are valid.

**Do**

Be encouraging and realistic. For example, if a friend is diagnosed with a terminal illness, listen to how they feel, encourage them to practice gratitude for the positive things in their lives, suggest effective mental clarity techniques and support programs. Work to enhance their lives *with* terminal illness rather than attempting to distract them or denying their situation.

**Don't**

Offer false hope or toxic positivity. Comments like, "just think positive!" or ,"it's not that big a deal," are not healthy or helpful. Suggesting that a person "positive-think" their way to health or saying things like, "Don't worry. We're gonna beat this disease!" does not promote progress of growth–the ultimate purpose of adversity. Stick to the concept that life itself is a journey. It is how we live that journey–with all its ups and downs–that matters.

## Learn More

For more information about the Six Steps, coming back from trauma, and renovating your life and business, visit:

*Deep Bench* with Todd Burnham on Apple podcasts, Spotify, Amazon Music, iHeart, and other podcast platforms.

**ToddBurnham.com**

# ACKNOWLEDGEMENTS

I grew up in the Valley, on the south side of Syracuse, NY. My mother, Nancy Burnham, was my hero. She was a social worker for New York State. We shared a rented duplex until middle school when we moved to the suburb of Fayetteville. Mom was a champion of the underprivileged, disadvantaged, and abandoned. She was a warrior of life, suffering from COPD for decades and maintaining a service-based focus. She was loved by so many, but none more than me. She taught me how to be a father by just being herself. I am who I am because of she, my Uncle Butch and my Grandmother Irene. That was my tribe. I miss my mom. Words don't work.

My wife, Katy, the love of my life and my Ambassador of Quan, has been by my side since the beginning of this personal and professional journey. She kept this crazy train on the rails with her patience, kindness, and positivity. Our marriage and my business have survived and grown stronger throughout our hardships. Katy, I love and adore you.

Our girls, Mae and Clara, have my heart and they know it. They are young warriors, both kind and fierce, and remind me daily that I'm not all that. I am so proud to be their Dad. Our sons, Archer, Noah, and Oliver are three amazing young men who are so very different in the coolest way possible. They have a stability, comfort, and happiness about them, certainly a result of their mother's influence. I am reminded regularly that Archer is a young version of me (especially when he hasn't slept).

Men in my life, who saved my life, and whom I admire. Robert Molyneaux, my paternal grandfather, a brick layer and laborer who taught me about pride. David Burnham, my father, who taught me life lessons by example. Tom Hall and Chris Kenneally, Fayetteville Manlius Boys lacrosse coaches, taught me about consequences. BJ O'Hara, my Hobart College Men's lacrosse coach, taught me that nobody is more important than the team. Jim Long, my friend and lawyer, a man who has done life right. Wally Morris (and Nicole), friends who taught me the answer to the problem of self-centered fear. Jeff Gosch, who gave me a glimpse of professionalism and friendship at a young age, helping me through some early *allegations* of wrongdoing. Jack Nielsen, the entire Nielsen crew for that matter, who believed in me and took me in when I was humbled but hungry. Brian Bagley, a friend who flew last minute to my mother's funeral to support me. Bill Krist, my West Genesee brother and golden retriever lover, a man that I love, admire, and respect. And Butch Walker, my uncle, the constant father figure in my life, who showed me what selflessness looks like.

My mother surrounded me with strong women. It's no wonder that the women in my life today are influential and strong. Katy is a beautiful peaceful warrior, and seeker of knowledge. Sharon Walsh, my godmother and mom's best friend, who exposed me to what a large family feels like and how family steps up when needed. Stephanie Randall, words can't express how much I admire you. You embody greatness and humility in how you lead, connect with and care about the people at Burnham Law. Mahalo for being in our lives. My grandmother, Irene Walker, the matriarch of my small family, who loved me so much she would let me win at Clue. My mother and grandmother taught me what it meant to be a family, to always protect it. I hope I am honoring them by sharing those same values with my children. Patty, Deah, and Brittany, my stepmother and sisters who are role models in their own beautiful, happy, and powerful ways.

And to everyone at Burnham Law: you can't fake culture and you can't fake wins. You all inspire me with your commitment to each other, to your clients and to your families. Not many want to live a life of service, let alone do so at the highest level and with the highest stakes, but you all do so with class and humility.